The
Miracle
of *Bubba*

An Inspirational Dog Story

JOE FLYNN

PAGE PUBLISHING, INC.
New York, NY

First originally published by Page Publishing, Inc. 2018

ISBN 978-1-64214-994-4 (Paperback)
ISBN 978-1-64214-995-1 (Digital)

Printed in the United States of America

CHAPTER 1

Meeting My Master

My name is Bubba. I am a black Labrador retriever with a very special story to tell. Allow me to start from the beginning to give you the opportunity to know me and my wonderful family. They are loyal and committed and chose me to be their new puppy. The people in my life, combined with my type of dog breed, became very important factors in my struggle to survive an extraordinary event.

I was born on a cold, blustery March morning in Orting, Washington, about an hour south of Seattle, with Mount Rainier looming in the background. My dad is a large chocolate Lab weighing in at an impressive 135 pounds of pure muscle. He held the title of being a famous, decorated champion bird hunter. My mom is a yellow Lab and a bird-hunting champion in her own right. Both were excellent at fielding birds, and it is in my blood too. They were raised to be companion dogs.

A few weeks later, nestled up with my brothers and sisters on a calm spring morning, I struggle for my mom's milk. As I am the runt of the litter, it is necessary for me to push and shove my puppy brothers and sisters in order to get my fair share of her warm milk. Her milk is delicious and satisfying. Using our soft fur to keep one another warm, we cuddle and squirm together.

Suddenly, I am lifted up and away from my mother. That's when I first meet my new master, Joe. He is tall with broad shoulders, big arms, and a powerful voice. He holds me high in the air and looks into my half-shut puppy eyes.

"Hi, little guy," Joe says in a deep baritone voice. I feel safe and secure as he holds me carefully with both hands. He twirls me slowly in a circle to view my entire tiny body. I peer back at him. We are high off the ground, as Joe stands six foot three. He has a big smile on his face. As I gaze upon his round red cheeks and curly brown hair for the first time, he passes me to his teenage son, Dan.

"Wow, Dad, this little guy has amazing fur! It's super soft and thick. I love his solid black color too," Dan says. Lifting me up to his eye level, he adds, "I've never seen a dog with blue eyes before."

They discuss that my mom and dad are excellent at searching for birds in the field. I am destined to be great when I grow up because it is in my genes too. Little did I know the importance of this fact and how it would eventually play an integral part of my life and whether I would survive a rare and extraordinary accident!

Joe seems like a nice guy. I sure do appreciate it when he puts me back down next to my mom. He is told he can come back in five weeks to pick me up. I am not sure where I will be going and don't care much because I just want more of my mom's warm, delicious, sweet-tasting milk.

The month of May approaches, and I am growing rapidly. The big day is finally here. It is time for me to leave the farm of chickens, cows, and horses along with my mother, brothers, and sisters forever.

On a calm, wet, foggy morning, as I play in the fenced area of the barn, I hear Joe's solid, unique voice heading in my direction. I stop in my tracks. As he gets closer to me, I see his big happy grin. He is alone.

"Hey, buddy, guess what time it is?" my master says while holding me tightly but gently.

Time for food? I wonder, staring at him blankly with my beautiful blue eyes.

He carefully puts me in a small crate with a blanket and secures the door. Next, he places me in the back of a big moving metal object with wheels that can roar really fast down the highway. This is my master's truck.

The loud noise scares me, and I feel alone for the first time in my life. On this day, I leave my mom, dad, and remaining brothers and sisters for good, never to see them again.

CHAPTER 2

My New Home

Turning eight weeks old and weighing fifteen pounds soaking wet, I am on the fast track to being very large. Everyone who meets me raves about my shiny, soft black fur. The feel of it makes you want to pet me all day long. That's okay with me.

The outline of my head is more block than round. The shape of my ears is perfect long triangles, velvety smooth and rather long. My nose is dark and fairly significant. My paws are large for my body, with toes arching out under my strong, growing feet. I am antsy and never sit still. "Go, go, go" is my motto!

Clumsy as can be, I run with exuberance everywhere. It is obvious I'll need some training and discipline to control my high level of energy.

I bark all the way to my master's house in that first truck ride. I guess it's the fear of the unknown plus leaving my family. Joe calmly reassures me things are going to be okay. He talks quietly, trying to calm me. Later, I learn this is what dogs do; we become part of our master's family, and if we work it just right, sometimes we can get the family to do whatever it is we enjoy doing the most. (More on that subject later.)

The big truck finally stops, and the engine is turned off. I am curious and trembling with anticipation. The kennel door opens, and I am gently set on the soft, wet lawn of my new home, absorbing all the unfamiliar surroundings.

Joe introduces me to his pretty wife, René. She is much smaller than Joe and looks like someone I can totally take advantage of. He explains this will be my new *mommy*. She seems like a softie. I'm hopeful I can easily get her to do just about anything for me.

A minute later, a tall fast-moving kid comes dashing through the side garage door. This is my new *brother*, Daniel. He is lanky and wearing a red-white-and-blue baseball cap. Still in high school, he plays numerous sports and seems to be constantly running in and out of the house. He has many places to go.

I should mention that Daniel is a new driver and will occasionally get into minor mishaps. This will divert my master's attention from some of my trouble-causing puppy years. Daniel and I have a lot in common. Both of us are usually tangled up in unfortunate situations.

The next day, my new sister, Shawn Nichol, comes home from college for the weekend. She is my new *sissy*. She is super pretty, with big blue eyes and long thick blondish-red hair. I love playing with her hair. She is away most of the time at college. When she comes home, she feeds me lots of treats, and I don't even have to do anything to earn them. Both Shawn and Dan are high-energy people, and that's good, because I am going to require a lot of everyone's time.

My new home is exciting to explore. There are ample rooms to go hide and play in and loads of places to go poop and pee to mark my territory. I definitely keep my new mommy busy chasing after me! I could always get myself into some kind of trouble!

After a couple of hours of my chewing and biting everything in sight, my new family decides to set up an enormous playpen in the family room. It's a six-by-six-foot area, and I can see everyone from this terrific spot. I am given a big brown teddy bear, a chew bone, and a ticking windup clock to entertain me while they tend to their chores and daily routine.

It's dinnertime, and boy, am I hungry! My master, Joe, bangs the food dish loudly as he pours just the right amount of puppy food into it. He is going to be training me to hunt and wants me to get accustomed to hearing loud noises while associating it with a positive thought. Nothing can be more positive than eating. Thus, as a puppy, I learn to associate loud noises with being fed.

Dogs are always trying to figure out the social order and where we fit into it. "Our dominance is greater than yours" or "your dominance is greater than ours" is important to us. This one fact will determine how well we listen to you. Joe chews some meat and then adds it to my puppy food. The scent of his saliva on my food sends a signal to me that he is at the top of the social hierarchy in my new family structure.

I am now nine weeks old and a wild, hyperactive, out-of-control puppy. I bark if I am ignored or left alone. René will hold me the most to get me to relax and settle down. As long as I am on someone's lap, life is good. My new home and family members sure seem really nice, and everybody makes me feel very loved and welcome.

My day gets very exciting when Master Joe comes home from work. I can hear his truck pull up in the driveway. His door slams shut, his car alarm beeping once to set. I count to ten really slow, and then he enters the front door. Party time!

Master Joe changes from his suit and tie to his jeans and T-shirt. I wait impatiently in my kennel. He always moves slow and methodical. I can hardly contain myself. Focusing my eyes on the stairwell, I patiently wait for my master to descend.

Finally, Joe clomps down the stairs from his bedroom. He kisses René hello while I watch with my head tilted. René likes to be in the kitchen. The smells are yummy. I'm getting hungry just thinking about it.

My master is better than anyone at releasing me from my cage and getting me to find or fetch something with a scent on it. Don't get me wrong—I really enjoy these little games of finding and fetching. No matter how tired my legs get, I want to play more and more. He understands this.

One of the first work tasks my new family teaches me is to fetch the morning paper from the end of the driveway. I love this because it allows me to leave the yard, put something in my mouth, and of course, get a reward. I receive a piece of beef jerky and plenty of hugs and praise to start the day. Usually, it is raining outside, so it's understandable the family will want to stay on the covered porch while I, in my goofy excitement, go get the paper.

My master stands by the *Seattle Times* paper in the driveway. His wife, René, is standing on the porch next to me, making sure that I obey the "Stay" command. Joe calls me.

"Here, Bubba."

And off I go running.

He kneels down, putting the paper in my mouth. René calls me back to the porch and has a delicious treat ready to give. I have to drop or *give* the paper to her to receive the treat. Every morning, I look forward to performing this task!

After realizing I'm going to be a very smart Lab, my new family discusses formal training for me. I am wild, energetic, and unfocused. A lot like my master when he was young.

CHAPTER 3

Puppy Years

Here I sit in the middle of a moist, grassy field. The wind is blowing slightly, and there are numerous smells circulating in the air around me. I need to focus on my master. The last thing said to me was "Stay," so I am to remain here. I try to move the first few times but I am immediately returned to the exact same spot and told to stay. When I am told to stay, it is said verbally and signaled by showing me the palm of the hand, sort of like a STOP sign.

Joe walks fifty feet away and is still showing me the palm of his hand. My muscles are beginning to tremble with anticipation of him dropping his hand and giving the "Come" command. Finally, the hand drops while he simultaneously says "Come." I sprint down the grassy field, feverishly exerting my leg muscles, until I reach the spot where Joe is kneeling. He praises me for a job well done. I love the pats and praise for doing good. We continue to practice this training in the field, with Joe increasing both the distance and the time I must hold in the *stay* position. I find this game to be both boring and repetitive, but I do enjoy the running and the amount of praise received. It is important to train any dog, especially a field dog and a family pet who will grow to be over one hundred pounds.

We follow up these training regimens with a fun game of fetch-and-retrieve. Today, Joe is adding a new wrinkle. We leave the grassy field and head over to the nearby lake. Joe brings a scented decoy. A decoy is a rubber duck or pheasant that resembles a real-life duck or pheasant. They both float if thrown in the water. Joe applies a scent to the decoy that is similar to an actual scent of a duck or pheasant. He has me stay on the beach while he tosses the decoy into the water. Upon its hitting the surface, he yells "Fetch!" and off I splash, focused intently on the decoy. What I fail to realize is that this is my first attempt at swimming. It feels natural, and I love it. The water is cool and refreshing. My long legs, large paws, and stiff, swinging tail rapidly propel me through the water. I grab the decoy softly into my mouth and head for shore.

Joe praises me for a job well done. He forces me to sit, take a breath, and stay while he throws the decoy into the water again. Upon its release, I am off again into the cool, refreshing water. I don't care too much for the *stay* or having to wait for the *release* commands, but they are important parts of the game if I am to become a good field dog. This game gets tiring. I never know when to quit and am sad when Joe signals it is over. My brief sorrow turns into a deep, relaxing sleep, with my long growing legs sprawled across the carpet in front of the fireplace. Members of my family will be vaguely talking in the distance, and I can occasionally feel them petting me, but I am catching some serious zzzz's.

Dan enjoys taking me up to the baseball park to watch ball games. Everyone loves to hold me or pet me. I always attract a crowd when at the baseball field. While everyone pets me, I am concentrating on the smell and aroma of the hot dogs and hamburgers being barbecued for the crowd. They even have bags of french fries.

When around or near cooked food, I tend to drool endlessly from my mouth. This isn't any ordinary drool, but a long spaghetti-type of hanging drool. It swings from side to side as I walk around the bleachers, waiting for any unsuspecting spectator to take their eye off their food while watching the game. I can strike as fast as a black belt ninja and eat a whole hot dog or hamburger in one bite. By the time the spectator finishes watching the play, they have no idea where their food has vanished. The only evidence is a string of my drool left in place of their food. Young kids walk by me looking one way while dangling their hot dog or bag of fries at my nose level in

JOE FLYNN

the other direction. In one bite, I can stealthily relieve them of their snack. It happens so fast they don't know whether to laugh or cry. Going to baseball games at the park is always a treat and a rewarding experience.

My vocabulary of the English language is growing rapidly. Besides the normal commands of "Sit," "Stay," "Come," "Down," "Up," "Fetch," "Heel, or "Bring," I am able to learn additional words or phrases. "Get the paper," "Let's go bye-bye," "There's Daddy," "Here comes Mommy," "Want a cookie?" "Where's sissy?" "Are you hungry?" (one of my favorites), "Go pee-pee," "Want to go for a walk," "Who is that?" and of course, "No" and "Bad dog." If my master challenges me to learn something, I always strive to please him by performing the task as taught.

My family thinks my intelligence has no boundaries while, at the same time, I am a dog—a puppy, no less—with a mind of my own. As good as I can impress you with the things I can perform for you, leave me alone for any period of time, and I can get myself into a lot of trouble too. I have chewed the wood off my doghouse roof in less than an hour.

One day, the new vacuum cleaner is left out while René walks across the street to have a friendly conversation with the neighbor. I gaze at the vacuum cleaner. It's like two gunfighters in the Old West standing out in the middle of the street, getting ready to draw on each other.

I completely chew the electrical cord off and into fifty different pieces on the floor. René is stunned when she returns while I am proudly sitting there, waiting for my next adventure. My tongue hurts for days after that debacle.

I love paper napkins because they have the aroma of food on them. I will eat a paper napkin anytime, anyplace, in a microsecond. If you place your drink on a napkin, I will sneak up next to you and snatch the napkin right out from under your drink. Sometimes I do it so fast that I will leave your drink still standing; however, there are plenty of times the drink spills and topples to the floor.

The family begins to teach me how to control all these wild and crazy urges I have as a puppy. Boundary lines are set within our house, and I need to abide by them. The kitchen and dining rooms are off-limits to me; however, if you leave that area, cross the boundary, and bring a snack into the television room, I consider you and the snack fair game. It is like being at the ballpark, watching a baseball game, as far as I am concerned. You have to keep your eye on me and your snack. On one occasion, it is a weekend and Shawn is home from college. It is late. Shawn and a few of her girlfriends arrive by taxicab. I can hear the doors of the cab shut in the driveway as they approach the door. How exciting! I get to smell and greet all of them!

"Shhh, my mom and dad are sleeping. I don't want to wake them up," Shawn whispers to her friends.

"Shawn, where is your closest bathroom? I need to go now!" one of her friends says while her other friends acknowledge they have to go too.

"Shhh, remember, my parents are sleeping. Bubba, get down," Shawn tells me as she scratches my head while I begin sniffing the group. I can smell their hamburgers and french fries radiating through the portholes of my nose.

"There is one bathroom on this floor and one downstairs. I will use the bathroom upstairs because my parents are sleeping. Remember to keep quiet," Shawn reminds them.

As they all disappear, I watch intently as they put the bags of burgers and fries on the hallway table. This table is clearly located on my side of the established boundary line in the house. As soon as the coast is clear, I ravish the bags, tearing into the food. In lightning speed, I devour each and every hamburger while scattering the fries across the floor. As the friends return to the room, I am halfway complete in finishing off the fries. Talk about a plan coming together!

"Bubba, what did you do?" Shawn exclaims as her friend's mouths drop open in disbelief and sorrow. "That food was our late-night snack! How did you eat it so fast?" she asks. "Oh, guys, I am so sorry. He is our new puppy, and a bad one. Come here, Bubba." Shawn hugs me while telling me what a bad boy I am.

After the late-night food incident, Shawn and her friends are always cautious when bringing any food into our house. That night, they all go to bed a little hungry.

On all my walks in the park or trips to the lake, I am trained to stay close to my master or family member. This has something to do with bird-hunting, whereby it is important for me to not wander beyond a certain distance. However, the side effect of this closeness makes me always want to be around a member of the family. If you are outside, I want to be outside. If you are in the house, I want to be in the house with you. If not, I may bark until you let me join you.

One afternoon, the whole family leaves to go to a wedding. One of René's sisters is getting married.

"Joe, be sure to leave Bubba in the house and lock the door. We are all ready to leave and waiting in the car," René instructs her husband.

Joe is thinking, *It is a beautiful early summer day. It will be nice for Bubba to be in the backyard.*

"Fine, honey, I will take care of everything. Hey, Bubba, come here. Come on, boy. Get in the backyard. You will like it more out here than in the house. It is too nice out." Joe talks to me while he locks the sliding glass door after putting me in the fenced backyard.

Joe heads out the front door to the driveway, where his family awaits in the car.

"Did you lock the front door? Is the dog in the house?" René checks with her husband.

"Yes, yes, everything is good. Let's get going," Joe answers.

So here I am in my own little backyard. *It will be hours before my family returns. What can I do back here to keep myself occupied in their absence?* My thoughts wander around in my head.

Let me see how deep of a hole I can dig. Here is a new flower plant René just planted last week in the yard, I think to myself then focus on it. It only takes me fifteen minutes to completely dig it out of the ground. Next to it is some kind of miniature Japanese tree René planted about six months ago. It looks like it is establishing its roots and growing well. It takes me a good half-hour to uproot this expensive little tree out of the ground. Once it's out of the ground, I begin to chew it into multiple pieces. This takes time, as the tree proves to be very durable. While it is still light out, I systematically move from each plant and small shrub René has growing in the backyard until I have all of them uprooted and chewed.

The last thing left is a cute little white garden fence René has installed to separate certain bushes and plants. I begin chewing and pulling on the different sections of this white fence until I have all the pieces spread around the yard.

Where is my family? When are they coming home? How come I did not get to go to the wedding with them? The thoughts spin around in my head as I patiently wait for their return.

Finally, the sun goes down and it is dark. It is getting past ten o'clock at night. It is a clear sky this evening. There are many stars up above. All of a sudden, this bright light begins to rise above the Cascade Mountains to the east of me. Why, it is going to be a full moon tonight! From where I sit on the back porch in our yard, I can watch the moon rise up over the mountains and shine right at me like it is staring me down.

"Urhrrrr, urh, urh, urhrrrr!" I begin to howl at the bright full moon looking at me. I have kept this up for over an hour when I see a police car pull up across the street. Looks like he is talking to one of our neighbors.

"Hi, Officer, I am the one that called. The dog across the street has been howling for almost an hour. I peeked over the fence, and it seems he is howling at the moon," the concerned neighbor tells the policeman.

"Do you know these neighbors? Are they home?" the officer asks.

"We don't really know them, and I don't think anyone is home," the neighbor responds.

"Is it normal for the dog to be out, making noise like this?" the officer further inquires.

Ignoring their conversation, I continue to howl at the moon in my best voice. Eventually, the police officer comes over to the gate of our backyard to see how I am doing. He looks in on me but decides to just leave a note on the front door of our house before leaving. I go back to howling as soon as he leaves. Twenty minutes later, I can hear the familiar sounds of my family's car coming up the hill.

"Okay, Shawn or Daniel, one of you let Bubba out for a walk. He has been in the house for almost six hours," René tells her kids while Joe hurries to be the first one in the front door. He wants to let me in from the backyard, but too late.

"Ruff, ruff, ruff, ruff, ruff," I begin to bark.

"Joe, did you leave Bubba in the backyard instead of in the house like I asked you to do?" René inquires.

"Honey, he is an outside dog. I am sure he had much more fun outside then he ever would have had inside," he responds.

Everyone has walked to the front door when René sees the warning from the local police regarding loud noises after ten o'clock at night. "Well, what do we have here, Joe? It is a written warning for Bubba howling for over an hour." René stares at her husband as she hands him the notice.

Dan lets me in the house, and I bolt up the stairs to greet my family. I am so happy to see them, especially my master, Joe.

"Hey, Bubba, get down, boy. Down, boy. What is this about you howling?" Joe says while rubbing my head. "Oh, honey, he probably just barked a few times. That's why it is just a warning." Joe defends himself and his dog to René.

"Well, let's see. We have five messages on our voice mail. Let me play them," René responds.

René cues up the voice mail to speakerphone and hits Play.

"Joe, René, I hate to be a bother, but Bubba has been barking and then howling at the moon for almost two hours. I figure you guys would want to know. Someone called the police, but that wasn't me. I am just leaving you this message. I came over to see Bubba in the backyard, thinking he might need water or something, when I noticed your backyard. Looks like he really misses you guys," a friendly neighbor's message plays on the voice mail.

René walks over to the outdoor light switch to the backyard and flips it on. She is speechless as she views my trail of destruction. However, the good thing for me is that it was Joe who made the decision to put me in the backyard.

Shawn leans over René's shoulder to look. "Oh my god, Dad, wait till you see what Bubba did to the backyard!"

"Joseph Patrick, look at what your dog did to my backyard garden! He has chewed and uprooted everything I planted in the last six months. My white fence is totally destroyed too!" René looks at Joe with that I-told-you-so look. My master is now on shaky ground while René decides his fate.

"Honey, I had no idea Bubba would do such a thing. I thought he would just sleep in the backyard until we returned home. Listen, I will get up early in the morning and clean it up, plus I will be happy to go to the garden supply store to find you some more plants," Joe says, offering his condolences.

In the morning, Joe rises early, makes coffee, and heads into the backyard with the wheelbarrow to clean up the wreckage. He finds two plants for salvage. The remainder head for the recycle barrel. Over coffee, René and Joe decide it is best not to replace the plants in the backyard. They feel it better to just have grass in the backyard until I can grow to be a little more mature.

Other things I love to do when in the house is crawling up on your lap and getting attention. Having you pet me behind my ears, eating fresh-cut grass from the lawn mower waste bag, and having you scratch my back. The most comical thing my family loves to watch me do is chase my shadow in the front yard and bark at it. On beautiful days when the sun casts a long shadow of my silhouette in the front yard, my family sits in their lawn chairs while I entertain them by playing an endless game of cat-and-mouse with my own shadow.

My puppy years are fun. I am getting to know and love my new family, and they are learning to love and appreciate me. My name, Bubba, sure fits my personality.

CHAPTER 4

My Field Adventure

A full six months old and weighing almost seventy pounds, I find myself sitting on a "Stay" command in the middle of a thick wooded, bushy field. Joe throws a decoy bird high into the air. I'm focusing with tunnel vision on the decoy flying through the sky when, suddenly, I hear a loud banging noise coming from behind me. Joe shoots off his shotgun. This is the loudest noise I have ever heard in my life. I sit perfectly still, with my eyes glued to the area where the decoy has landed in the brush.

"Well, excellent stay and focus, Bubba. You might be a really good one," says Joe before releasing me.

I dart across the field, jumping over bushes and fallen branches while keeping a trained eye on the high grass where I saw the decoy fall to the ground. The scent from the decoy is strong in the tall grass. I weave back and forth, sticking my long black nose, sniffing into the brush. Finally, I snatch the decoy softly up into my mouth and head back to Joe. While praising me for its retrieval, he serves me a small dinner right there in the field. What a treat! This cements the sound of loud noises as a regular phenomenon into my repertoire. After I have devoured this small dinner, we continue to play this game for over an hour in the field. I sit and stay while he throws the decoy, blasts the shotgun, and releases me to fetch it. The noise of the shotgun becomes second nature to me and an integral part of my learning to hunt.

Then comes the second phase of this interesting new game we play in the field. While lying in the wooded field on a "Stay" command, Joe puts a towel over my head so I can't see, then he takes a scented decoy pheasant and hides it in the field. This is much different from finding a scented decoy in the house or the yard. There, the scent is strong and dominant. Here, the wind is breezy and the scents of other animals are mixing in the air. All my training has been with this one scent, so I labor and focus all my sniffing ability on the scent of the decoy. I am bred to be a bird-hunting dog. I come from a long line of dogs that possess a heightened sense of smell, focus, energy, and awareness.

Joe comes back, uncovers my head, and releases me to go find the *birdie*. This is the name he gives to the scented decoy. Little did I know, but this would become my most favorite game and, over the years, my master and I would play this game often. But getting back to today . . .

Off we go looking for the decoy birdie in this large open wooded field. I traverse back and forth in front of him, every so often picking up a weak, light scent of the decoy bird. The more we look, the stronger the scent becomes, until now the scent is almost as strong as when I smelled it up close with the towel over my head. Suddenly, I discover the decoy in the bushes. I am excited, my master is happy, he congratulates me, then as I sit there, my master throws the decoy bird high into the air and he makes a loud bang with the firing of his shotgun. As the decoy hits the ground, I rush to fetch it and receive unending praise. The game rounds off my training for hunting birds in the field.

I am still in my puppy years, a full seven months old. My body has grown long and large, but I still have much filling out to do and, at times, am rather clumsy. My baby-blue eyes have changed color to a beautiful golden brown. My master, whom I now will refer to as Joe, and I are up early, getting ready to go on our first real hunt together. He is dressed in some fancy, new clothing that is primarily the color of orange. He even has an orange-colored collar for me to wear. We pack up and I jump into the back of his truck, but for some reason, I notice that he is not taking my favorite game toy, decoy birdie, with us. I sadly see decoy birdie hanging in the garage as we drive away from the house.

Usually, when we pull into the parking lot of the wooded field where we play decoy birdie, we are the only ones there. Today, there are fifteen trucks or more, all with masters with orange clothing, and each of them has a dog like me at their side. There are black Labs, yellow Labs, chocolate Labs, German shorthairs, and more. The weather is a typical autumn day in the Pacific Northwest, with a low cloud cover, overcast, and a slight breeze blowing. Listening to all the other dogs while observing the area, I feel the excitement in the air just to be here with their masters. I, too, become excited, but I am not quite sure why yet, as I have yet to see anyone with a decoy birdie to play with.

The masters and their dogs line up at the edge of the wooded field, waiting for the clock to strike eight o'clock sharp. No hunters or dogs are allowed in the field until eight o'clock in the morning. Among us dogs, we can hardly wait—the excitement building within us to be released is unbearable. Then all the masters give the release command with instructions to go find a birdie. Off we run, smelling through the tall grass and bushes, back and forth in front of our masters, then bingo, I smell the scent of the decoy birdie. I wonder, how did my master get the decoy birdie out here without me seeing him? Who cares? The scent is getting stronger and stronger. Joe is close behind, watching, when I discover the scent is coming from under a bush right in front of me. I stop and hover over the bush, dripping with anticipation, which is overwhelming all my senses. I stay standing perfectly still, focusing on the bush, and literally, time stood still for an eternity.

Then Joe says, "Birdie, Bubba."

I pounce on the bush with my two front paws, and suddenly out flies a large birdie, bigger than the decoy birdie, straight into the air. There is a bang from Joe's shotgun, and the large birdie heads for the ground about thirty yards away in some thick brush. I run to the spot and start searching through the thick brush for the birdie. Upon locating him, I softly caress him in my mouth and bring him back to Joe. He congratulates me for a job well done. He explains to me that this birdie is called a pheasant.

Later that night, while I lie on the carpet floor in front of the crackling fireplace, I can see Joe and his beautiful wife, René, making a special dinner called wild pheasant. They make a big fuss about this dinner, taking time to prepare it by blending the wild taste with onions, spices, herbs, and vegetables until the pheasant is cooked to perfection. They celebrate this milestone occasion with lighted candles and a bottle of red wine.

Dreaming of more but exhausted from all the running around from the day's excitement, I am very content. What a fun and exhilarating day!

CHAPTER 5

Learning the Outdoors

My master plans a special event for us in Eastern Washington. It is wintertime and especially cold on the other side of the mountains. There is half a foot of snow on the ground, with temperatures in the low thirties. It is just Joe and I hunting the banks of a half-frozen streambed. We have been at it for a few hours with no luck when we round the bend of a stream that opens up into a small picturesque lake. The winter scenery in this neck of the Cascade Mountains is much to behold. The fresh snow creates a winter wonderland for the eyes to devour. Curiously I wander out onto the partially frozen surface of the lake, and before Joe can call me back, the ice beneath me shatters. I plunge into the cold, freezing water. Joe attempts to come toward me but quickly retreats as he is too heavy for the thin ice. He calls for me to come. Numerous times, my front paws break through the ice as I attempt to crawl back onto the frozen surface. Every failed attempt submerges me back into the frozen water.

Joe attempts to slide out onto the ice in a prone position to get close enough to grab my collar. His attempts fail as the ice starts to crack underneath him, forcing his withdrawal. Finally, I get my two front paws onto the ice while kicking with my rear legs. The ice breaks away again—only this time it slices open my right paw pad. The ice is as sharp as a broken piece of glass. Kicking frantically, I successfully haul myself up onto a solid slab of ice. My paw bleeds profusely. Joe motions me over, and I maneuver off to the side and to the safety of the bank. As I shake the freezing water off my coat, Joe tries to examine the depth of my cut paw. He pulls out his reading glasses to get a closer look.

"Bubba, this cut is deep. It is going to require stitches to properly close it," Joe says, letting me know.

First things first, we are three miles from where we parked the truck. Needing to hike back down a deep, snow-covered forest logging road, Joe rips away his white T-shirt from underneath his clothing and ties it tightly around my right paw. Off we go. I limp next to my master down the road. Eventually, the blood bleeds through the T-shirt, leaving a stain in the white snow as we hike back to the truck.

Upon arrival, Joe wraps me in a thick blanket, and off we go to find a vet. We stop in Ellensburg, Washington, at a vet clinic. Joe has called ahead, so they know what to expect. The lady vet and Joe are standing together while I lie on a table.

"Mr. Flynn, this cut is deep. I need to completely clean Bubba's wound before stitching it up. We will need to put him under as this can tend to be painful. Help me keep this mask attached to his nose and mouth. It will pump oxygen mixed with enough gas to put him to sleep," the lady vet explains to Joe.

"There, he looks like he is out. I will administer a local pain medication directly to his paw to anesthetize the area." She continues her explanation to Joe while sticking a syringe needle directly into my severed paw.

Yikes! That sent a chill all the way up my leg into my body! I yelp in my dreamlike state while levitating my entire body off the table.

The vet doctor reaches for the gas dial and spins it to maximum, releasing a large dose of gas into the oxygen mixture. I immediately go transcendental into a deep sleep.

"Wow, that was fast!" Joe comments.

"He has enough in him now to anesthetize a horse. He shouldn't stir again for over an hour. He shouldn't have even felt the needle with what I originally gave him," the doctor opines.

She works feverishly stitching up my wounded paw, with Joe standing over my unconscious body. Finally, she finishes her work and says, "He will be out for at least another hour, and I would like him to stay here until he recovers his consciousness."

"Okay, my daughter attends college here in town at Central Washington University. I am going to go pick her up, grab a cup of coffee, and come back," Joe tells her.

"First, help me move him onto the bathroom floor. There is rug in there where he can comfortably lie until he awakens."

Joe and the doctor move me into the bathroom and close the door.

I wake up twenty minutes later. Groggy, I stumble into the metal trash can, knocking it over. The vet doctor opens the door and says, "You should not be up yet with what I gave you."

I have a cone contraption around my neck and head. It restricts me from being able to chew away the bandaging to my right paw. They walk me outside in my drug-induced state and put me in an outdoor kennel to await my master's return. Shawn and Joe are surprised to see me outside as it has only been forty-five minutes since he left. He thought it would take an hour for me to wake up. I am sure happy to see them, especially Shawn. I miss my sister, Shawn. She is always giving me treats and cuddling me.

The doctor gives Joe instructions as to my continued care and comments on my high level of energy and strength.

"Your dog seems to have an extremely heightened level of energy. I work equally on both dogs and horses at my country vet practice. Your Bubba was more like treating a horse in the way he recovered from his drowsiness."

Over the years, we have many hunting excursions to find pheasant, and each of them is memorable and exciting. It is a special time we have together, bonding in the outdoors. There are too many of these trips for me to write about individually, but generally, we combine pheasant-hunting in the early morning with duck-hunting at midday and into the afternoon.

Pheasant hunting involves the two of us combing miles of brush in the field for two to three hours, then at midday, we go down to the river. Here we strip off the hunter orange, hide it, and set up a camouflage spot on the bank of the river. Joe brings out his folding chair, and we eat lunch together at our favorite spot on the river. Hunting ducks down by the river just requires me to sit next to Joe, waiting for a duck to fly by. If we are lucky, and I mean lucky, a few would eventually fly by, presenting a difficult crossing shot. If he hits one, it usually lands in the river, and this is the fun part for me. Tired from the full morning of pheasant-hunting, I am always willing to brave the cold water of the swift, strong river current to fetch the duck.

When either pheasant or duck is brought home and cooked for dinner, Joe and his wife, René, will always make a special occasion of it, out of respect for the bird or duck, while I relax and sleep on the carpet in front of the fireplace.

On another occasion, Joe takes me steelhead-fishing. Prior to me, he had another black Lab named Blackie. Joe and Blackie never hunted together, but he took Blackie river-fishing. Joe would wade out into the cold winter river in his full-body neoprene waders to fish for steelhead. Blackie would stand on the toes of his boots, leaning up against his legs in the current, watching Joe continuously cast for steelhead salmon. When the water was too cold for him, he would return to the beach and watch from the shore.

I am just under a year old. It is a cold winter day, and Joe is going steelhead-fishing, so I tag along. Joe has me stay on the shore while he wades out waist-deep into the river. He starts casting upriver, letting the current drag his line downriver through the bend, then pulls and recasts the line upriver again. I watch him repeat this maneuver over and over until, all of a sudden, a salmon splashes out of the water. It flies high into the air then performs a dance on its tail across the water before diving below into the depths of the river. It rapidly pulls line out of Joe's fishing reel.

Stay or no stay, I want to go investigate. I run into the river. Joe focuses on netting the live salmon he has on his line and hasn't noticed me until I swim past him. He says, "Bubba, the current is too strong and swift. Get back here." I swim to the spot where the salmon last disappeared underwater. I feel a strong force pulling me downstream. I look up, and Joe is now in the distance upriver. I can see him heading for shore. I swim as hard as I can to get back to Joe, but the cold winter current of the river continues to pull me quickly downstream. Joe is no longer in sight. The river bends back and forth through the forest, and I am pulled along in the swift-moving current. As I round the next bend, the river widens and straightens out. I can see my master's truck on the riverbank in the distance downstream. He has driven his truck downstream on an adjacent gravel road then waded partially out from the shore, whistling for me to come. Swimming diagonally toward him, I swiftly drift in the strong downstream current. Slowly I can feel the current start to release me as I make my way toward shore. Joe grabs my collar, pulling me the rest of the way to the bank of the river.

I shake off the cold water after traveling over a mile downstream in the freezing winter current. It is almost as cold as the frozen lake water. Joe is glad to have me back but upset with me too.

"Bubba, what were you thinking? We are going to have to work on the 'Stay' command more. If there weren't a gravel road running adjacent to the river, you could have been swept away or lost." Joe speaks to me while scratching my head.

He saw that day what a good, healthy swimmer I am. It will forever leave a mark in his mind of my high level of energy, strength, and endurance.

It was the last time he ever took me fishing too.

CHAPTER 6

Over Four Years Later

I am a full-grown, five-year-old adult male black Lab. My legs are long and muscular. I can run, jump, or swim with tremendous power and stamina. Until now, we've discussed hunting with Joe, but I go to the park or the lake with René and sissy, Shawn Nichol. They take me to the park or lake to run, smell, and fetch ball. I develop strong ties with all the members of my family. They run me until they are exhausted. I always want more. Dan takes me for long walks in the park. The whole family knows I need plenty of exercise as it seems I have an endless supply of pent-up energy.

Dan moves to Montana to attend college and recently joins the Army Reserve. Not too long after joining, he receives orders to deploy to Iraq in support of the war effort. This means we will have a houseguest for the eighteen months while Dan will be away, his dog, Keely. Dan rescued her from the animal shelter in Bozeman, Montana. She was a bit frail and thin when he first adopted her. She had been living on the street for the first eight months of her life, fending for her own food. She had roughed it through a cold, harsh mountain winter roaming the streets of Bozeman, Montana. A frail 75 pounds when Dan adopted her, she has since developed into a large 120-pound female Saint Bernese Mountain dog. Her presence can command attention, and she enjoys stealing all of it when she is around. The thing I adore the most about her is when we are each given a bone, I chew mine in a matter of minutes, which is what I do with all types of food, but she daintily plays with her bone. Upon licking and savoring her bone for a short period, she buries it in the yard in a shallow grave. She never does quite figure out that I have a nose capable of smelling and finding just about anything. When she isn't looking, I go and uncover her bones and eat them. Later, I always see her wandering around the yard with a puzzled look on her face.

Today is the day we are sending Dan off. He has been home for a few days to drop Keely off and say goodbye to his family. His army unit has orders for deployment to Iraq. Keely and I have met before on a few occasions when Dan brought her home from school for a short visit. She is a wonderful dog and easily loved by all that meet her.

The family gathers in the truck, with Keely and me in the back, accompanied by Dan's army duffel bag and backpack. I hear Joe and René talking before Dan comes out of the house. It is going to be a trying day for them. It is not every day that parents drive their son to the airport to catch a flight off to a war. I can see and feel the tension in both of them. Their moods are subdued. There is a history of service in the family. Joe's grandfather was a World War I veteran, his father was a decorated combat veteran in World War II and Korean War, and Joe served four years in the USMC and is a Vietnam era veteran. Now Dan will be serving his country, doing a tour of duty for Operation Iraqi Freedom for the US Army.

As we drive to the airport, the conversation is quiet and simple. Dan promises to write and keep in touch. René sits next to Dan so she can both feel and be close to her son for the drive to the airport. When we arrive, Keely and I say our goodbye in the parking lot. Dan hugs us both and tells Keely to go easy on me. Joe and René escort Dan inside the airport.

They want to appear strong to Dan in their sendoff, but we dogs can feel when something is bothering a human. They give off a signal, and I sense it. Keely senses it too. Inside, they come to the security checkpoint, where they have to say their final farewell to Dan.

Joe says, "Dan, be sure and give your mom a big hug, then save a little something for me."

René has tears flowing down her face while she bids her only son farewell, wishing and praying he will return safe from his tour of duty.

"Son, we love you, I love you. We are proud of you. Take care of yourself. Now, give me a hug." Joe chokes out his words.

The long line of passengers to enter the security checkpoint can easily see this is a family sending off a soldier, not just to catch a flight to another US city, as most of them are doing. Two parents embracing their uniformed army son off to Iraq. The moment captures all the passengers in the vicinity. The line parts, allowing Dan to cut through after saying farewell to his family. René and Joe hug each other and look on until he disappears through the security checkpoint.

They walk back to the truck embracing each other. René has tears flowing down her cheeks, and this is the first time I have ever seen my master with a tear in his eye. It is a quiet, solemn ride home.

Keely and I spend many evenings lying on the carpet, competing for Joe and René's attention, which, I must say, she is quite good at, stealing the show. She has been staying with us for going on six months since Dan headed off to Iraq. My sissy, Shawn Nichol, who has graduated from college a few years before, has a new dog, Benji. Benji is a small American Eskimo mixed with a Lhasa apso. *Wow, is that a mouthful!* He weighs fifteen pounds soaking wet. When he comes to visit, he and Keely play nonstop together.

The big news buzzing around the house is, Shawn Nichol is getting married to this terrific guy she met while away at college, Brent. He is a smart, athletic guy and, at times, goes bird-hunting with Joe and me. The wedding plans are on for this September, and Dan may even be coming home from Iraq on a week's leave for the wedding, so there is lots of hustle and bustle around the Flynn household in the months leading up to the wedding.

I am getting cheated out of some of my trips to the park or lake for exercise. Then one afternoon in late June, while Keely and I are in the front yard, I see Joe pull in the driveway in his truck. He exits his truck, and I have a ball in my mouth, ready to play some fetch. Little did I know the importance of what would happen next!

CHAPTER 7

Tragedy Strikes

This is the day that is going to change my life forever! I run up to Joe, prancing around him with the ball in my mouth. *Give me some attention! I want to play!* We exchange greetings. Keely is given a lengthy massage when she rubs up against him. She can always find a way to steal some affection from you. Now she is content and meanders back to the front porch for a nap. I continue to circle Joe with the ball in my mouth. This is a ritual I have performed many times with him. I run around him on the front lawn with the ball in my mouth until he says, "Gimme that ball, Bubba!" And I then flip the ball into the air from my mouth in his direction, and he catches it. "And let the games begin!"

Joe tosses the tennis ball lazily across the front lawn. With a burst of speed and all my energy, I run to fetch the yellow tennis ball. It hits the lawn and bounces upward.

Suddenly, I find myself crashing down onto the moist grass, sliding sideways to a complete halt. I feel a sharp pain erupt in my neck. I yelp before collapsing powerfully to the lawn. My entire head and body lay glued to the ground. I lie motionless and helpless on my right side. The yellow tennis ball is a few feet in front of my nose. I send signals to my body to move so I can retrieve it. My legs and body are powerless. I cannot budge a muscle. As I am apparently completely paralyzed from the neck down, my eyeballs and tongue are the only things shifting.

Joe approaches me and kneels down by my side. "Hey, what happened, boy?" He thinks I have simply skidded sideways and will jump right back up. In reality, I've collapsed like a sack of potatoes falling from the sky.

Keely senses something is wrong. She moves close and begins circling me. She moans and cries, her instincts taking over, and she starts licking me.

Joe begins slowly stroking my head gently. He feels my chest with his other hand. My heart is beating incredibly fast.

Keely continues to moan excessively, so Joe escorts her into the house. Time to think fast—René won't be home for a few more hours. He tries to move me, but at 125 pounds of deadweight, I am too heavy to lift. He stands up to ponder his next step. At that exact moment, a silver Toyota 4Runner is slowly driving down the hill past our house. Joe recognizes it to be our neighbor Mark, who is a retired veterinarian.

Before Mark can close his vehicle door, Joe runs up to him. Mark can tell by the concerned, desperate look on Joe's face that something is seriously wrong. "Hey, Mark, my dog collapsed a few minutes ago." Breathing heavily, he adds, "Can you come over and help? I need to know what to do."

Mark quickly hops out of his car and says, "Let's go." Mark is a calm person by nature, and his composed personality and professionalism instantly relieve some of Joe's anxiety.

As I lie helpless, I can see Mark and Joe standing over me. Joe describes how he saw me collapse. Mark kneels next to me and begins examining different parts of my body with his hands. Mark is puzzled. He knows me to be a big healthy young dog. He asks Joe, "You sure he didn't hit anything?" Joe confirms that I hadn't, just collapsed.

Mark thinks, *Strangest thing. No movement. No response. Zero motor skills. Bubba is still breathing strong.* Mark unclips his cell phone and calls a local Redmond vet clinic. He knows the vet doctor there. He coolly explains the situation in a few brief words. It is only two miles away. They discuss the importance of keeping my neck and spine supported. Any slight movement can have disastrous results and can further harm me.

Mark thinks it is best to try to minimize any movement of my body. They bring the stiff, hard aluminum dog ramp out of the truck and slide me on it then use their belts to secure me to it. The ramp serves as a stretcher, and I am loaded into the back of Joe's truck. Mark wishes us well, and off we drive to the local vet clinic in Redmond, Washington.

Upon arrival, Joe goes inside and returns with a vet doctor and two assistant technicians with a stretcher on wheels. I am strapped onto the moveable stretcher for my safety and rolled into the clinic. Blood tests are taken and x-rays performed. I have not sustained any trauma (direct injury to my body from an outside source), there are no bones broken or injured, and everything seems in working order, except I am completely paralyzed. The staff empties the exam room to leave Joe and me alone with the doctor.

I look over and can see the concern on Joe's face. He is being told that there is nothing further that can be done for me. The doctor says, "Mr. Flynn, we don't know why your dog collapsed. We can surmise he suffered a major stroke of some sort. Your dog is completely paralyzed and will not be able to recover. The best we can offer you is to put him down. Euthanize." A term that means "to cause death painlessly, to end suffering."

Joe asks, "Is Bubba in any pain right now?"

"No, he can't feel anything from his neck down. He has lost all his motor skills," the doctor replies.

Joe says, "I need to call my wife and daughter before I can make any final decision."

The doctor understands and tells him to take his time and use this room to make any calls. "Just have one of the technicians come get me when you are ready."

CHAPTER 8

Consulting the Family

Today happens to be Shawn's twenty-fifth birthday. She is on the phone with her mom.

"Happy twenty-fifth birthday, dear daughter! Are you ready for your special dinner tonight? I made your favorite cake with vanilla frosting and sprinkles!" René excitedly tells Shawn.

"Oh, Mom, I'm on a diet for the wedding!" Shawn eagerly replies.

"It's all healthy. I used applesauce instead of oil, egg white, and low-fat cream cheese for the frosting." They both prefer dessert over the main course. The lower the fat and calories, the more they can eat. They will just work out more at the gym this week.

Changing the subject, René inquires, "How is your handsome fiancé?"

"Brent is doing better. The Achilles surgery went well. I can't believe he popped and shredded it. They did win the basketball tournament, though. I guess he took one for the team!" Shawn continues, "His brother will get him from the hospital to his condo later today and up the big flight of stairs. He needs to sleep and rest for a couple of days. It is only two more months until our wedding. He better be able to walk down the aisle. He is not going to get out of saying 'I do.'"

"Come over as soon as you can and get ready to be pampered. We have a few presents for you!" René excitedly says. "I'm in line for the ferry and will be home in a couple of hours. I had a nice visit with your grammy."

"Where is Dad?" Shawn asks.

"He mentioned going to Hartmann Park to watch baseball. Bubba and Keely are at the house, waiting for you to bring Benji over. They'd probably enjoy a good play at the park. It is a nice day for it too!" René casually replies.

"Okay, Mom, see you around six o'clock tonight. Love you!" Shawn hangs up.

Back at the Redmond vet clinic, Joe is left alone with me and slumps down in a chair to take a deep breath. He pulls out his cell phone and calls René. No answer. He then hits speed dial for Shawn.

"Shawn, it is your dad. Do you have a minute?" he asks.

"Hi, Dad, what's wrong?" Shawn can tell by the quiver in her dad's voice that something is up.

"Bubba had a serious accident, and I can't get ahold of your mom. She could be on the ferry coming back from visiting your grandma." Joe's voice trails off.

"Is he going to be okay?" she demands.

"How is Brent?" Joe replies, remembering his future son-in-law has just had surgery.

"He is fine, Dad. We're taking him home soon. His family will be around tonight and tomorrow to take care of him. What's going on with Bubba?" Shawn asks, keeping him focused yet wanting to help.

"It's bad. He had a major stroke and collapsed. He is completely paralyzed. We are at a Redmond vet clinic, and there is nothing they can do for him. I am sorry, for it is your birthday and all. I am in the room with Bubba. He is just lying on a stretcher. The doctor is waiting for me to call him back into the room. I am going to have to let him go, honey."

The news crushes Shawn as her dad's voice quivers.

Shawn says, "I want to come see him before you make any decision."

Just then, there is another call ringing in on Joe's phone. "Shawn, your mom is calling in right now. Let me take her call and then get back to you. I won't make a decision until I talk with you again," he says.

"Hi, Joey! The ferry is just landing in Seattle. I have a few errands for Shawn's birthday tonight before I'll be home. Do you need anything?" René says.

Joe sighs. "Bubba had an accident. I am in Redmond, at a vet clinic. It is really bad. We are going to have to let him go!"

René is both stunned and puzzled. "Did he get hit by a car? Weren't you watching him?"

"No, honey, it is the strangest thing. He just collapsed on the front lawn. Mark came over to help me, and even he said he has never seen anything like it before. They have taken x-rays and blood tests here. They are just waiting for me to call the doctor back in the room to give the approval to let him go. I was on the phone with Shawn when you called. She is crushed. I am, too, for that matter." Joe struggles to communicate.

René is thinking then speaks. "Talk with the doctor again and check if there are any other options. I am sorry, honey. We all love Bubba, but I know you are really close to him. I know you will make the best decision for him." Now René's voice stutters in sorrow.

"Listen, call Shawn for me. Tell her not to come. This is going to be tough enough on me to do as it is. I will see you at home later." Joe says goodbye, and René hangs up too.

Joe requests the doctor to return. They speak for ten minutes. The doctor closes by saying. "It is a long shot. Whatever happened to your dog must have something to do with his nerve system. We just don't know much about it at the regular vet level. There is a clinic in Lynnwood that has performed work and research on the canine neural nerve system. I would be giving you false hope to tell you they can cure whatever has happened to Bubba, but they may have some answers for you."

Joe responds, "Listen, I am too stunned at this point to just give you the go-ahead to put Bubba down. My wife and daughter are upset over this too. It is so sudden for us. I think I would like to go up to this Lynnwood clinic even if it is just to get some answers. It will give my family and me time to come to grips with the decision we have to make. Can you call them for me and have your staff assist in getting Bubba back out to my truck?"

The doctor agrees, makes the call, and has his staff assist me.

Shawn is calling in. "Dad, I just got off the phone with Mom. I want to come down there to be with Bubba before you do anything."

Joe stops her. "Honey, honey, just wait a minute. Bubba and I are leaving this clinic and heading up to a clinic up your way in Lynnwood. They have done some work on dogs with neural nerve system problems. I don't want to give you too much hope, because he is really bad, but we might at least get some answers. It is a shot," Joe says.

Shawn thinks and says, "Dad, I've heard of this place. It's not an ordinary vet clinic. It is a major trauma center for pets. People bring their animals from all over Washington, Oregon, Idaho, Montana, and even Canada to this place. They handle serious cases and can handle three to four major operations at once. It will be a really good place for Bubba. They will help him."

"Honey, like I said, Bubba is in a really bad shape. Please don't get your hopes too high," Joe reiterates. "Okay, honey, I will give you a call back once we get going from here. Say a prayer for Bubba, and let us hope for the best."

Shawn signs off from the conversation with her dad, but she can hear her big, strong dad sinking into despair by the tone of his voice.

Before we leave the Redmond vet clinic, the doctor tells Joe, "Listen, it is a really hot day out today. It has now been a few hours since Bubba has gone down. He has water hydration needs that need to be addressed within the next hour. Keep him cool while transporting him to Lynnwood, and make sure he starts to get some water once you arrive there."

The emergency clinic in Lynnwood, Washington, is twenty miles north. He has me securely loaded into the back of his truck on a stretcher. He collects all my x-rays and blood test results while paying the bill for $700. We head for the Last Chance Dog Hotel.

CHAPTER 9

Lynnwood Trauma Center

Joe calls René back while he is driving to Lynnwood. "René, it is me. I am on my way up to Lynnwood." He explains all that transpired between the doctor and him at the Redmond clinic. He goes over his reasons for taking me to the Lynnwood clinic and how they specialize in neural problems with canines.

She asks, "Do you think he has a chance?"

"Look, like I told Shawn, he is really bad. The doctor in Redmond thinks we might at least get some answers in Lynnwood. Let me have the staff in Lynnwood examine Bubba. It will give us a second opinion, and I just need some time to deal with this," Joe says.

René can hear in her husband's voice how he is struggling to deal with losing his best friend. She knows more than anyone how close we are. "Honey, I love you. Call me as soon as you know something. I am stuck in traffic in Seattle. There must be a ball game tonight. I will be at home later."

According to the x-rays, mechanically, all is in perfect order. I have no broken bones, no trauma to any part of my body. I did not collide with an object. I should be able to get up and just walk or run right out of the vet clinic. René is deeply troubled by the news and understands if Joe has to make the decision to let me go. She is puzzled as to the suddenness of this bad news. I am not some old dog that just limps around the house, with my days numbered. An hour before, I was healthy. Neither Joe nor his family have had any time to prepare for the abruptness of my situation, yet now they have to make a decision regarding my final outcome.

Upon our arrival at the Lynnwood Vet Center, technicians come out to the truck and load me onto a moveable stretcher. It is a hot June day, and the half-hour it takes to drive here has really made me thirsty. I am starting to dehydrate. There is a sorrowful, concerned look on Joe's face when they move me past him into the emergency room. This is no ordinary vet clinic. It is a major trauma unit for pets. It is the Last Chance Dog Hotel. The worst of cases arrive throughout the day or night. It isn't uncommon to have three or four major operations going on at once.

"Mr. Flynn, we'll need you to sign some paperwork," a staff member explains to Joe. "Here is an estimated cost sheet for you to approve, showing the low to high end of fees."

Joe studies the paperwork. This veterinary emergency center specializes in neurology. This branch of medicine deals with the structure and function of the nervous system. The diagnosis as to cause and reason for my disorder is going to cost a pretty penny. The estimate ranges from $600 to $3,000 for a mere twenty-four-hour period.

"Mr. Flynn, we have three emergencies going on right now. We will fit Bubba in as soon as possible. In the interim, we will stabilize him by starting a drip solution to hydrate him and insert a catheter to handle the discharge of his urine."

Joe asks, "Is he in any pain?"

"No. He still has pain medication in his system from the Redmond vet clinic, according to his charts. If you can please complete and sign off on the paperwork we have given you, we will take Bubba in the back," the administrator instructs.

Joe signs the paperwork while I think, *How will he rationalize the $700 he just spent in Redmond and now this emergency clinic? Am I worth it? Can I be saved? Can I be a normal dog again?*

As I am wheeled to the operating rooms in the back, Joe is told he must stay in the front waiting area. Only staff is allowed in the trauma area. There are two large dogs, each on a different operating table. Both were hit by cars. They have broken bones, lacerated cuts, and bruised internal organs. They are each in a fight for their lives. One will be saved, but the other's injuries will overcome him and he will die on the operating table. Their masters are in the waiting room area with Joe. This is not the time for visiting or holding my paw. I am on my own.

Technicians quickly tend to me. An IV tube is inserted to administer fluids and a urine catheter to aid in my urinating. I am being stabilized and prepared for my examination.

Joe sits patiently in the waiting room area. The room is fairly large. There are at least a dozen chairs and a few small sofas. There are boxes of tissue located strategically around the office. Peaceful music plays in the background. Although the environment is calm, people are constantly coming and going through the front door. Three receptionists man the phones and the incoming guests with pets, all while handling the clients checking out too.

Joe observes his surroundings. A young man is comforting an elder woman who is coming to terms with the news that her beloved dog will not survive. Her companion of only eight years was struck by a van, and he has severe internal injuries. I watch him die on the operating table while awaiting my turn for my examination and diagnosis.

I am afraid.

Sitting in the waiting area are a couple in their midtwenties. Their toddler runs around, using the various furniture pieces to balance himself. The young lady is visibly upset. Their new Persian cat has been attacked by two coyotes. She retreats to the restroom to compose herself. When she emerges, a doctor approaches them. Their feline is too badly injured and cannot be saved.

Time slowly passes. Shawn has not arrived yet.

My initial examination is complete, and Joe is brought into the room to discuss my fate. I have tubes running into me when Joe walks into the room. He walks over and pats me so softly, telling me to rest easy. He wants to know if I am in any pain, and he is assured that I am not. He talks with my new doctor at Lynnwood.

"Mr. Flynn, I am Dr. Johnson," says the doctor.

"Please call me Joe," he replies.

"Bubba's examination is complete. Let me discuss his situation with you. We have narrowed what happened to Bubba down to one of two things. He either has a dried-out vertebral disk in his neck that burst or he suffered what we call an FCE stroke. Either of which caused his full paralysis. In order for us to ascertain which one it is, we will need to run an MRI scan on him. Before we go to the MRI scan, let me discuss both the dried-out disk and FCE stroke with you," says the doctor.

"They are both serious situations for Bubba. The first, it is possible he had a dried-out vertebral disk in his neck. This disk, through his ongoing movements, finally hit a breaking point, burst, and shattered into pieces, thus causing his paralysis from the neck down," says the doctor.

"What can be done for him if that is the case?" Joe inquires.

"It is really a new area of surgery in canines. It will require surgery to attempt to fuse the neck together and then long-term care. He will have to be immobilized for a period of time, then a long road to rehabilitation to walk again. I can go into this further for you if the MRI scan determines this to be the cause," says the doctor.

"I am not going to do neck surgery on my dog," replies Joe. "Tell me about this FCE stroke."

"Stands for fibrocartilaginous embolism. It is basically a stroke in the spinal cord instead of the brain, whereby a microscopic piece of fiber cartilage broke free in Bubba's bloodstream, travels at a high rate of speed, punctures through the blood vessel, and enters the spinal cord in his neck, causing an embolism. The result is spinal fluid and blood loss leaking inside his body," continues the doctor.

"What can be done for Bubba? What can we expect if this is the case?" Joe inquires.

"Dogs who suffer this type of stroke experience partial temporary paralysis to their limbs usually for two to three weeks. Then all or part of their ability to move their limbs again comes back gradually over a period. They need to be rehabilitated with therapy. However, Bubba is the most extreme case we have ever seen. We usually only see partial paralysis to one or two limbs. His is a full paralysis to the whole body from the upper neck region down to the tip of his tail, and 98 percent of large canines that experience FCE strokes are euthanized. I want to be straight with you relative to Bubba. He will be a long shot. It will take months of care and therapy only to find out along the way that your dog will be too crippled to learn to walk again," says the doctor.

"In order to determine what caused this to Bubba, would you have to perform an MRI? How much would the MRI cost?" Joe asks.

"Yes, to determine the cause, we need to do the MRI. Due to the swelling and blood under the skin on the left side of his neck, we will have to wait three days before administering the scan. It will cost $1,200 for the MRI plus the maintenance of Bubba for the three-day period at $100 per day. Additionally, you have incurred an estimated $500 for Bubba's examination," the doctor replies.

Joe sinks down in his chair as he ponders both options. "Listen, I told my daughter I would not make a decision until she arrives. Can you give me some time to think until she gets here?"

"Yes. There is a private room off the hallway with a phone in it you can use. I will instruct the front desk to have your daughter escorted back here when she arrives. Once you decide, just ask one of the technicians for me, and I will return," says the doctor.

I can see Joe is devastated, by the look on his face. He walks out of the room to await the arrival of Shawn. He thinks, *What a complete loss to such a healthy dog!* The room he waits in is adjacent to where I lie belted to my stretcher, immobilized.

Sissy arrives and is shown into the office where Joe is sulking. She knows her father to be a strong, confident, and positive man. She walks into the room and looks at her father and sees the defeated look upon his face.

"Oh, Dad, I am so sorry about Bubba! Where is he? What are the doctors telling you here?" she asks.

Joe looks down, hands Shawn some tissues, and says, "Honey, Bubba is through that door. Go see him. One of the technicians or doctors in there can answer your questions."

When Shawn comes through the door, she is crushed by the sight of me helplessly lying there. I am unable to acknowledge her presence in anyway. I can't lift up my head, wag my tail, whine, or cry, as even my throat is paralyzed. I want to acknowledge her. She pats me and hugs me. She is visibly shaken and upset. The technician in the room discusses with her that my condition is grave, options not too promising, and that a decision needs to be made. Shawn returns to the room where Joe is waiting, sobbing uncontrollably.

"Oh, Dad, his condition is so bad. It is such a freak thing to have happen to him," she says, sobbing.

Joe consoles her. "In life, honey, sometimes things really unexpected happen. There is no explanation for why they happen either, they just do. This will not be easy for me to decide today, but we need to let Bubba go. Did you say goodbye to him?" Joe asks.

Just then, René calls in. "Hi, Joe, I am at home. What have you found out?"

They speak for a few minutes while Joe brings her up-to-date as to the two potential causes, the prognosis for both, and a summary of all the costs.

Shawn leaves the room to come see me and say her final goodbye.

She cries while hugging me. "Oh, Bubba, I love you! You were always such a good dog and friend."

I wish I can acknowledge her in some way, but I just lie there immobilized. She leaves the room in tears while stopping to tell her dad she can't be here any longer. It is just too hard on her emotionally. She is leaving to be with René.

René tells Joe, "Bubba has been a great dog and family pet. Do what is best for him. We will support you. I love you, honey." René says goodbye.

Joe is now alone, pondering my fate. He walks back into the room to gaze upon my crippled, paralyzed body on the stretcher. He asks the technician if he can please get the doctor. The doctor returns.

"Doc, can you please educate me more fully on this FCE stroke. Is there something I can read to have a better grasp and understanding of it before I make my final decision?" Joe inquires.

The doctor opens a book, and Joe reads over the following.

What is a *fibrocartilaginous embolism* (FCE)?

- FCE is the functional equivalent of a stroke in the spinal cord rather than the brain.
- It is a sudden blocking of an artery or vein of the spinal cord by a clot of foreign material.
- FCE is often associated with strenuous exercise and/or trauma. It can appear rapidly without any warning. After the initial pain of trauma, an FCE is not painful but can cause weakness and paralysis (inability to move).

Causes:

- The cause of FCE is thought to be a small fragment of intervertebral disc material that enters the spinal cord's blood supply.
- This causes a varying degree of damage that is dependent on what part of the spinal cord is affected.

Clinical Signs:

- Signs can affect one or several limbs of the body. These signs can range from gait abnormalities to complete paralysis, with fecal and urinary incontinence.
- FCE signs develop over a moment, minutes to hours, and typically stabilize within the first twenty-four hours.
- Pain may be present immediately following the embolic event but then subsides.

  After initial medical management, intensive nursing care and physical therapy are required. The goal is to maintain muscle tone while the spinal cord tissue heals.

Prognosis:

- The severity of neurologic dysfunction, the amount of disc material that has embolized, the degree of accompanying spinal cord swelling, the location of the spinal cord infarction, the overall physical condition of the patient (dog).

  In general, the ability to perceive deep pain in the affected limb(s) and tail remains the major prognostic indicator. Even if paralysis is complete, *the perception of deep pain remains the key* to determining if permanent damage has occurred. This means that, even if paralysis has occurred, if the conscious perception of deep pain is intact, a functional recovery is anticipated. The time required for recovery and the degree of neurologic improvement are quite variable. Two to three weeks to begin recovery with most or a portion of clinical function restored by four months. Diligent physical therapy and good nursing care are important for recovery.

He asks the doctor, "It states here the importance of the ability to perceive deep pain is the key to determine permanent damage. When are you able to determine this perception of deep pain?"

"That is an observant question. If the MRI determines the cause to be FCE, then it can take two more weeks to make a determination as to Bubba's ability to perceive pain," replies the doctor.

"Look, I am emotionally spent and fatigued at this point, and so is my family. It is my daughter's birthday today, and we are having a little celebration for her tonight. I don't want to leave here and have to tell her we put Bubba to sleep. Additionally, I want to know what caused this to Bubba. Let's go ahead and schedule the MRI scan for him three days from now. If the MRI determines he has a burst disk in his neck, we will have him put down. If it is the FCE stroke, we can discuss at that time the possibility of a recovery plan," Joe concludes.

Joe hugs me. I am wheeled away. They add a liquid steroid and an anti-inflammatory to my drip solution. Lying on a blanket off to the side of the operating room floor, I feel completely alone in my new world. I await the results from my MRI test in three days.

CHAPTER 10

MRI Test Results

Joe arrives home. His day has been long, dramatic, and grueling. René, Shawn, and Joe somberly celebrate Shawn's birthday. All are drained from the day's events. The only good news Joe can give is that I am stabilized and still alive, at least for three days, while we await the MRI test results.

Late that night, René and Joe discuss my situation.

"Honey, what made you decide to keep Bubba alive today?" René asks.

"It is not so much that I decided to keep him alive as it is that I couldn't let him go. It all happened so fast and suddenly. I know the MRI test is expensive, but it gives me the time to come to grips with the situation," Joe responds.

"Listen, I want to visit him tomorrow. I want to observe first-hand his condition. Bubba was—I mean *is* our family dog. I want to be involved and supportive," René says.

The next morning arrives early in my new home. It's sterile and empty, and I lie completely limp on the side of the operating room floor atop a pile of thick cotton blankets. My head is propped up with a synthetic pillow. I feel alone as I wait for someone to remember I am here.

Everybody on staff knows I can't move a muscle. I can see and hear the staff moving about the room. Hungry for food and starving for attention, I pass the time with mini naps. My eyes lazily roll open, and I can see two staff technicians observing me.

"I just came on duty this morning after my two days off. What is the case with this dog?" inquires the technician.

"He came in yesterday in the early afternoon, and his name is Bubba. He is completely paralyzed from the neck down. We are to stretch and flex his legs every six hours while flipping him over to his other side every two hours. He is scheduled for an MRI in two more days," says the technician named Jennifer.

"What is his prognosis?" asks the technician.

Jennifer replies, "He has a neck injury from a shattered disk or a major stroke. Both are really serious."

"Is the owner of Bubba going to try to keep him alive?" asks the technician.

"Hard to say. I know for sure, if it is a shattered disk, he will be put to sleep. If it is a stroke, I'm not certain," Jennifer replies.

"Were you in the room with the owner yesterday when he came in? Did you observe the owner?" the tech asks.

"Yes. He was really close to putting him down. I think he is just waiting for the MRI results before he gives us the go-ahead to do it. You know how dog owners just need time to deal with it," Jennifer says.

"Let us just do our job, then. It's sad, though, as he is such a beautiful dog," the tech replies.

They finish exercising my limbs and carefully roll me over to my other side. The technicians see a large amount of tragedy at this clinic. It is hard for them to get personally involved and attached to a dog. They must remain professional while performing their jobs. They finish with me, and I am alone again.

What's happened to my old life? No one is here for me. I miss my family, and I am very scared. I need to be back at my house with Master Joe and my family. I even yearn for my friend Keely girl. I crave my spot on the couch to rest on.

I doze off again into a deep sleep.

As I awake, I find myself strapped down on the moveable stretcher, again being rolled into a visiting room. René comes to see me for the first time. She enters my sterile room. I don't even flinch. Afraid to touch me, she sits in a chair, facing me. My eyeballs look in her direction and then droop. She observes me motionless.

Tears quickly flow down her face.

"I'm sorry, Mom," I want to tell her. But all I can do is lie still.

"Oh, Bubba, how did this happen?" She wipes her face, but the tears keep flowing. She moves closer to me within inches from my face. I can feel her warm breath linger across my nose. I can smell her familiar scent as only my eyes can roam in their sockets.

"I'm looking pathetic, Mom, I know," I want to say. "Please don't cry."

She gently strokes the soft area between my eyes. *That feels good, Mom. Please don't leave.* I look up at her to see if she can read my mind.

"Bubba, this is worse than I thought." She is sobbing more now. She gets tissue to wipe her eyes and nose. She uses multiple pieces of tissue to keep up with her steady flow of tears.

"You look awful, boy." She wonders if I am suffering. "No wonder your dad is down in the dumps." She looks up toward the ceiling. "Please, God, if there is anything we can do for Bubba, please let us know."

As René leaves the clinic, she calls Joe on his cell phone, but it is turned off. He is downtown in a business meeting. Frustrated that Joe is not available, she calls Shawn at work.

"Hi, honey, do you have a second?" She holds her breath in case Shawn is too busy to chat.

"Yes, Mom. It's so insane here. I was just going to take a break. Did you go see Bubba?" her daughter's comforting voice inquires.

"His condition is terrible, much worse than I could have imagined. His whole body is damaged from whatever happened to him. I don't know how he can come out of this. It was awful to see him so helpless," her mom voices while being clearly upset.

Shawn remembers her first visit to me yesterday, and tears return to her eyes. "Mom, I know it's bad. I try not to think about it. Have you talked to Dad?"

Impulsively and out of frustration, René goes into a full rant. "You know your dad. I think he is in denial. Bubba is a huge dog, literally, with damage to his whole entire body. I can't take care of him. We've spent a fortune getting tests done, and it scares me to think how far your dad will let this go. He always has a never-give-up attitude. He thinks he can fix everything. I can't believe he thinks Bubba will recover from this. It's insane!" René comes up for air. "Sorry, honey, I know you're at work."

"Mom, just say a prayer. It's okay. I know how Dad can be, but in the end, he will be logical. Don't worry, it will work out," she sweetly says. "I'll call you tonight after I see Bubba." She starts to whisper. "I've got to run. I love you."

"Love you too, Shawn. Thanks. Bye."

It takes three days to get me ready and schedule the MRI test. I continue to lie immobilized on the floor, watching the comings and goings of all the different types of dog injuries that transpire in my new home. Many are hit by cars, run over with broken bones. Some are operated on and fixed; others are injured so badly that the best that can be done is to relieve their pain while their owners prepare themselves to say goodbye to their best friends.

The technicians are like clockwork. Every two hours, they flip me over to my other side, and every six hours, no matter the time of day or night, they exercise my legs by stretching and flexing them. Jennifer is the one I like and get to know the best. She talks calmly to me while exercising or flipping me over, and when she has a spare moment, she comes by just to see how I am doing.

My master, Joe; his wife, René; or my sissy, Shawn, comes to see me for an hour each day while I await my MRI test. René's first visit to see me is traumatic for her. She goes home telling Joe she cannot see any hope for me. She tells Joe she hopes he does not let me suffer in this condition for very long. René really loves me, and we have spent quality time together around the house over the past five years. Joe works and travels for days at a time with his job, so René and I have formed a special bond. I follow her around the house or sit next to her for hours at a time in her home office while she works on the phone. I can always get her to take me to the park or the lake for some fun. My situation is tough for her to take. All are stunned by my utter physical demise. From a healthy, athletic specimen in one moment, and now to this immobile, paralyzed dog. They know that as much as everyone loves me, they are most likely going to have to let me go.

I hear Joe say, "I at least want to know what happened to him before we put him down."

Thus was his thinking when he ordered the MRI test for me. It is a way for him to come to grips with the decision he knows he will inevitably have to make while giving every one of my family members, except Dan—he is in Iraq—a chance to say goodbye.

Most dogs are given a drug to make them sleep in order to keep them immobile for the administration of the MRI test. I haven't moved in the last three days, so it is not necessary for me. I lie perfectly still while this big machine goes back and forth over my body, scanning me to find the trouble spot. I am hoping the test will determine that I have a massive stroke versus a vertebral disk bursting in my neck, as I heard my master say that he will definitely not let them perform a neck operation.

I hear the technicians talking to each other as they move me to a visiting room to get the results of my MRI test with the doctor and my master.

"Well, Jennifer, any word on the owner of Bubba?" asks one of the technicians.

"The doctor wants me in the room when she goes over the MRI results with him. I am hoping for the best for Bubba. I started to let myself get attached to him," Jennifer responds as they wheel me into the visiting room.

"Hey, good luck with this dog. We have to make the rest of the rounds this morning. See you at break. We can talk then," the technician states as he leaves the room.

It is just Jennifer and me in the room together. She leans over me while softly stroking the top of my head. "Bubba, the doctor and your master should be here shortly to see you. I hope we have some good news for you today," she whispers.

I have been expecting the whole family to come today, but only Joe arrives. He walks into the room. He greets Jennifer and scratches me smoothly between the ears.

"Hey, boy, how are you doing today?" Joe asks as Jennifer leaves the room to go get the doctor.

I am happy to hear his voice, but I can tell his mind is occupied and his tone is guarded.

The doctor and Jennifer return to the room together with the photo image results of my MRI test.

"Hi, Mr. Flynn, I am Dr. Johnson, and I will be going over Bubba's MRI test results with you today, but before we get to that, let me review with you his condition. Bubba's urine is very dark, which indicates he has a bladder infection. We have been treating that with antibiotics for two days. It should run its course in two to three more days. Additionally, he has been running a fever that was caused by an ear infection. We have cleaned out his ears and treated the infection with antibiotics too," the doctor states.

"We have had Jennifer and a number of our other technicians exercise and flex Bubba's limbs at four different intervals during the day and night to keep any muscle atrophy from establishing itself. He has been on a diet of water solution mixed with steroids and an anti-inflammatory, vitamins, and a liquid food supplement. The goal is to keep him hydrated and sustained while trimming him of twenty to thirty pounds. Which brings us to his MRI results," the doctor continues as Joe listens intently.

"Take a look here at the MRI photo," the doctor says as she points with her pen to an area in my upper neck region. "Bubba experienced an FCE stroke in the upper neck area of his spinal cord. This dark area is blood and spinal fluid loss that has bled out within his body. Now I know Bubba hasn't moved yet, but as his body heals itself, he will start to recover some movement to his limbs. How much of his ability to walk or run again is uncertain at this point. His stroke was massive, and it involves his whole body. The MRI indicates his left side may be worse off than his right side." The doctor pauses while taking a breath.

"Listen, I read through the materials you gave me the other day and went online during the last three days to educate myself further on this canine FCE stroke. Does he have a chance at recovery?" Joe asks the doctor.

"A chance, yes. Will it be a long road to recovery? Yes. Can you go down the recovery road and find out weeks later that Bubba's body can only partially recover from the effects of this stroke? Yes. It is too early to tell what the long-term effect will be on Bubba. Bubba is still a healthy, muscular young dog. If he is to have a chance at recovery, it will be necessary to maintain him until his body can start to heal. As he heals, he will begin to regain movement to some or all parts of his body. If he does regain movement, he will need to be given rehabilitation therapy. To measure his recovery can take two to three weeks. If he does recover enough movement to his limbs to walk again, rehabilitation therapy can take an additional two months or more," the doctor answers as Joe listens intently.

I can see the puzzled look on Joe's face as he stares at the floor. All this news is exciting to me, because just then, I release a solid bowel movement onto the stretcher. The doctor, Joe, and Jennifer look over at me as the smell captures the room.

Jennifer states, "I will take care of that. It is actually a good, healthy sign that his system is working well." Jennifer grabs a plastic bag to gather up and clean off the stretcher.

"You know, Doc, I came today with a shovel in the back of my truck to go bury Bubba on the bank of a river. It is one of our favorite hunting spots. Over the years, we spent many great moments there together. My wife and daughter couldn't come today knowing what the most likely outcome is going to be. If you can tell me that, in two months, I can have my old dog back, or even a good part of him back, I can buy off and go down that road. However, it sounds like I will be just postponing the inevitable." Joe speaks, thinking out loud.

"Logical thinking. All that you say can be true. Rather than biting off and making a decision for one, two, or three months, why don't you consider making a decision for two weeks? If you can financially support Bubba for two more weeks at $700 per week, this will give his body time to heal. We will have a better understanding as to the depths of the injury to his body and be able to give you a more-informed prognosis regarding his recovery," the doctor states as Jennifer looks on.

"Can you give me a few moments with Bubba to process and think through what we just talked about?" Joe requests.

"Sure thing. Jennifer will be available just outside the room for you. Just let her know when you have decided, and she will get me. If you have any other questions, please don't hesitate to ask. We know this has been hard on you and your family over the last three days." The doctor shakes hands with Joe as she leaves the room.

Jennifer tells Joe she will just be down the hall to the right when he is ready. She pats me on the head and gives me a hug as she leaves the room.

One of the technicians familiar with my case sees Jennifer walking out of our room down the hall.

"Jennifer, what gives with Bubba?" he asks.

As Jennifer turns and looks up at him, he sees the tears in her eyes.

"Hey, what is going on with you?" the technician asks Jennifer.

"I let myself get attached to this dog. Dr. Johnson just went over the results of the MRI with Bubba's owner. The prognosis isn't the best, and he came by himself, without his wife or daughter. He even stated he has a shovel in his truck to bury Bubba along some river," Jennifer tells him.

"Wow, it is never good when they come by themselves. Listen, you and everyone here have done the best we can for the situation. You have to let it go if that is the direction the owner is going to take. You know that!" The technician tells Jennifer.

It is just the two of us in the room together after the doctor and Jennifer leave.

"Bubba, you are making this hard on me. You know I want to do what is right by you, but I have to weigh all the facts. The problem is, I consider you my best friend. I spend more time with you than anyone else. You have always given me your unquestioned loyalty," Joe says while reminiscing over all the hunting trips and evening walks we have taken together over the last five years.

I would love to be able to just give him a sign, move something to give him some hope, but my body just lies limp on the stretcher, I think.

"Well, I have one thing I have always relied upon in life when I am faced with a difficult decision. It was drilled into my head as a young USMC Marine to never quit. Find a way to keep going forward. I am going to let that principle decide what we do here today," Joe decides as he moves toward the door to find Jennifer.

"Jennifer, can you and the doctor please return to the room?" Joe requests.

The doctor and Jennifer come into the room together as Joe stands alongside me.

"Listen, I am going to make the decision today to give Bubba two more weeks."

Jennifer's eyes light up as she listens to Joe talk.

"If, after two weeks, there is no measureable improvement to his condition to lead us to believe he can make a recovery, then I will have you put him down. In the meantime, I want your staff to use all your talents to give him the best of chances to recover. I will stop by the front desk on my way out and take care of the $1,400 to cover the next two weeks."

"Mr. Flynn, I think you made the best decision possible under the conditions. It is a difficult situation. We will monitor Bubba closely daily. We will strive to give him the best chance possible at recovery. As always, you and your family can visit him every day," the doctor replies.

Joe thanks the doctor and Jennifer then rubs my head and gives me a hug before leaving the room.

When Joe is in the parking lot, he sends a text message on his cell phone to René and Shawn. "We are keeping Bubba going for the next two weeks. Let us pray for his recovery."

CHAPTER 11

The Critical Next Fourteen Days

66 Hi, Dad, it's your daughter. I just got your text message. What is going on with Bubba?" Shawn asks her dad.

"Well, I didn't want to call from the clinic until I made the decision to move forward with Bubba. I do need to talk to your mom in person to explain my reasoning, and I am going to need your total support with your mother about maintaining Bubba for the next two weeks. She thinks I am incapable of making a logical decision with him. Partly, she may be right, but I want to go with this, give it some time before making any final decision," Joe responds, strategizing with his daughter.

"Dad, I am happy you decided to give Bubba a chance. I will support you with mom big-time," Shawn tells her father confidently.

"You do understand he is a long shot and we are going to be in uncharted waters? We can get a few weeks down the road only to learn that he won't be able to recover," Joe reiterates strongly to his daughter.

"Dad, let us just focus on giving Bubba the best opportunity possible during this two-week period," Shawn says.

"I hope your mom will be as understanding with my decision as you are. She is worried about planning the wedding, and I might bring home a large handicapped dog to care for in the midst of things," Joe thinks out loud to his daughter.

"Dad, just focus on the next two weeks when you talk to her about Bubba," says Shawn.

"Okay, wish me luck. I have to run. Love you, honey." Her dad signs off.

"Love you too, Dad." Shawn hangs up.

Later that same day, Joe arrives home. René is in the kitchen, in the middle of cooking dinner for the both of them.

"Hi, honey, did you get my text message?" Joe asks.

"Yes," René replies.

Joe ponders her one-word response before asking, "Do you want to discuss the reasons behind the decision I made today regarding Bubba, our family dog?"

"Why didn't you call me from the clinic to discuss it before you decided?" René inquires while facing away, busily stirring the vegetables on the stove.

"Because I knew you would probably not agree with my decision to maintain and keep Bubba alive. I know he may be a lost cause and it can be just a waste of our money to prolong his life, but I feel it is too early to decide. I want to give his body a fair chance to heal. The doctor will have a more-informed perspective and prognosis in two weeks' time," Joe says, pleading his case to his wife.

"How many things in life have you quit?" René asks.

"What does that have to do with Bubba?" Joe asks, answering a question with a question.

"Everything—you don't quit things! You keep plodding away endlessly. There are times in life when you have to make a judgment. Are you capable of making that decision when it comes to Bubba?" René asks.

Joe sits silently and thinks before responding to René.

René speaks further to him on the subject. "Joe, I can't have you bring Bubba home and expect me to have to carry him outside to go to the bathroom. He weighs as much as me. Our house has steep stairs. He can't walk right now and may never be able to walk again. Your work requires you to travel. Who is going to help me move a large handicapped dog in and out of the house?" René stops to catch her breath.

"Listen, honey, I agree with you. I won't bring him home unless he recovers and can walk again under his own power," Joe promises her.

"What is the timeline for you to decide that? Two weeks, one month, two months? How long and how much more money will we have to spend before you can make that decision?" René gazes directly at her taller husband.

Joe pauses for a moment and remembers his daughter's advice to focus upon the next two weeks.

"Well, I only approved the next two weeks. If, after this period, the doctor can't give us a favorable, optimistic report toward his recovery, I will be prepared to make the necessary decision. He is my dog and our family dog. You have to go with me on this and give me your support." Joe finishes his sentence and looks at his wife in the hopes of gaining her support.

René ponders their conversation while putting the final touches on dinner. She asks Joe, "Do you want to open a bottle of wine and pour us each a glass for dinner?"

"Sure. We have a bottle of white and red, which would you prefer, honey?" he responds.

"White is fine," René answers.

They sit down and enjoy a nice dinner together. Shawn calls later in the evening to voice her support for me. René is on board for the next two weeks. My mommy has always been the glue holding things together at the household.

My new home at the twenty-four-hour vet clinic is very interesting. There is never a dull moment around here. The staff and the doctors are very professional, taking great pride in their work and the care of us, their patients. Whether resetting broken bones to performing major operations on internal organs, they are top-notch. This team of professionals will definitely give me a fighting chance for recovery.

Every two hours, they flip me over from one side to the other. Every six hours, they bend and stretch my legs in order to exercise the paralyzed muscles. I can see my legs move when they bend them, but I cannot feel anything. Periodically, I smell an aroma of food coming from the staff lunch break room. My nose is still working perfectly. I want to go investigate, but the commands from my brain to my legs don't register. My new world involves me observing movements, smelling the different odors and scents that swirl around me.

Once a day, they put me on a stretcher and wheel me into the visitor's room when my master comes to visit. Often, sissy comes with him, as they work together a couple of blocks from the vet clinic. René comes once or twice per week, as the Flynn household is located twenty miles away. René works part-time retail in Seattle a few days per week too. So with traffic, household to run, and Keely to care for, it is more difficult for her to come see me. On one occasion, when René and Shawn come to visit me, they have to wait for an hour only to be told that due to the emergency cases having to be handled, they cannot spare the technicians to move me to the visiting room. René is struggling with the seriousness and hopelessness of my situation.

The technicians are great. Jennifer rallies all of them to get personally involved in my success. Ever since Joe has made the decision to give me two extra weeks, I've become everyone's goal. The technicians squabble over who is going to get to care for me and exercise my legs. Jennifer is the lead technician assigned to my case, and she loves every minute of it. Numerous times, she spends her break time with me, talking softly to me while giving my legs some extra stretching and bending.

I can hear Shawn, Joe, and René talk about how they must do everything they can for me during this fourteen-day period. They want to give me the best chance of surviving. They work hard exercising my legs during their visits, but I can see from the expressions on their faces the odds are long toward my successful recovery.

On one visit, Uncle Bob comes to see me with my master. Uncle Bob works with Joe. I know Uncle Bob from numerous bird- and duck-hunting adventures. Bob is an accomplished outdoorsman and fisherman. Today, he comes with Joe and is devastated to see me in this condition. Bob knows me from running through tall grass, jumping over bushes, or swimming across swift-moving rivers during our hunting excursions. Joe explains to him what happened so that he will be prepared upon seeing me; however, Bob has a look of sorrow on his face. When Bob goes home later that night, he tells his wife how distraught he is over what happened to me. He feels and thinks Joe is hoping for the impossible. He tells his wife, "I think Joe will end up having to put his dog down very shortly."

Each of the fourteen days passes by—visit after visit, my family all coming to see me. On one visit, my master has just completed his first successful run of a marathon race (twenty-six miles). When he is sharing this news with me, he tells me, "If I can get my fifty-two-year-old, 230-pound body to do a marathon, then we are going to find a way for you to walk again." My master is a former USMC sergeant and has a no-quitting mentality.

On another visit, René comes with her friend Kate. René and Kate enjoy playing tennis and going hiking together. They are both in tears, as it has been over a week now and I haven't made any progress or showed any signs of moving my legs. Kate has just seen me for the first time and is overwhelmed by my total incapacity. She knows me as this muscular, athletic dog that prances and romps around the front yard whenever she comes over to our house. The sorrow on their faces is tough to look at, but I am still excited for their visit. It is nice to see and smell the familiar faces and scents of my family and friends.

Otherwise, I am on the floor with my blanket inside the Last Chance Dog Hotel operating room. I am starting to bond with the technicians that are exercising and massaging my legs every day, especially Jennifer. Everyone involved is determined to give me the best opportunity to succeed at a recovery. If we fail, it isn't going to be because no one tried. I really miss eating; however, the liquid food solution with the proper proteins is sustaining me, and it is accomplishing my doctor's goal of reducing my body weight. They want my body weight down to 95 pounds from the 125 pounds that I tipped the scales at upon reception. They are quickly accomplishing their goal, as I have lost 15 pounds since coming here. They feel that if and when my legs regain movement, it will be better if they only have to support 95 pounds versus 125 pounds.

All in all, we are progressing through the fourteen-day period, but still no movement. Finally, the two-week period is up, and although everyone has done their very best, I have lost close to twenty pounds, I have retained my muscle tone, and no muscle atrophy has set in, there are still no signs of movement.

My master comes for this visit by himself to meet with my doctor. He has a serious look on his face. Jennifer, one of my favorite technicians, is in the room with us. The doctor explains that, in some cases, it may take a little longer for the body to show signs of recovery. The doctor is going to perform a paw pad nerve test, which involves the doctor grabbing the largest black paw pad on each of my legs and pinching it. The goal is for me to yelp in pain when the doctor pinches it. The perception of deep pain will confirm that there is still a neural connection intact from the bottom of my paw to my brain. The doctor starts by grabbing my rear right leg paw pad, as it is the farthest from the point of my injury to the left side of my neck. The doctor squeezes hard, and I feel some pain and yelp. She proceeds to my right front paw pad and squeezes hard, and I yelp again. Then she goes to my left rear paw pad and squeezes hard. I can feel a dull sensation, but no pain. She tries a second time on this leg, squeezing extra hard, and now I feel some pain and yelp. Finally, she goes to my left front paw pad, closest to my neck injury. She has to squeeze extra hard, but on the third try, I can feel it and I yelp.

The doctor explains to my master that even though I haven't moved my legs yet, the paw pad pinch test establishes there is still a neural connection from my brain to the bottom of my paws. The stroke affects my left side more than my right, but there is a possibility that I can, given time and intensive therapy, recover movement to my limbs. I must be excited at this news, because I let go of a nice bowel movement right there on the stretcher. What a sorry sight I am in my master's eyes! Little did I know, this is decision day—my master has brought his shovel with him again for that beautiful riverfront burial site.

Jennifer cleans me up while the doctor explains to Joe it is understandable no matter what decision he is to make regarding my fate. He has given me much more of an opportunity than most dog owners would have done in a similar situation. The doctor leaves the room in order to give Joe time to decide my outcome. Am I to be euthanized today or possibly be given a few more days or a week to show signs of recovery?

Jennifer speaks to Joe. "Look, Mr. Flynn, I may be overstepping my bounds, but if you will allow me, I would like to say a few things on behalf of Bubba."

"Hey, you and your staff's performance have been outstanding. I am here today and at a crossroads regarding a decision for Bubba. Two weeks ago, I was here with a shovel in my truck to go bury him in one of our favorite spots, and today, that same shovel is back in my truck again. It cannot get any tougher, so please speak freely. If there is ever a day to speak your mind, now is the time," he responds.

"Like the doctor said, no matter what decision you make here today, you definitely went beyond what most owners would do for their dog. The other technicians and I were impressed when you decided to give Bubba the fourteen days two weeks ago. I have talked to your wife and your daughter when they have visited. I know your family is torn over Bubba's condition, but let me tell you, there are six technicians working extra hard on Bubba around the clock, trying to get this dog back up on his feet. If you can just find a way to give him a little more time to heal. I know you have to make a decision, but I want you to know there are five other technicians waiting for me to come out of this room. Basically, Bubba's team here at the clinic wants to know if they can have a little more time." Jennifer ends her impassioned plea by walking out the door with tears in her eyes.

You see, most dogs that come to this clinic are repaired and sent home or they don't make it. It is unusual to have one stick around like me. The technicians have developed a bond with me and realize the difficult odds I face. They know this is decision day for me, but they don't want my corner to throw the towel in yet.

Joe and I are in the room by ourselves. He speaks to me about how we are at the end of the road. He struggles with letting me go but thinks it is for the best; however, in the back of his mind, Jennifer's speech gives him pause.

Joe's phone rings; this time, it is sissy, Shawn. She wants to know what decision Joe is making, and she tells him, "Dad, if the money is playing a part in the decision, we can make cuts to the wedding. We can slash some things to allow enough money to give Bubba a chance."

Joe thanks Shawn for calling and tells her, "Honey, your support with Bubba means a lot to me. You know what he means to me. Now I need to be able to think, so let me go. Thanks for calling. I love you."

Shawn is sobbing when she bids her father farewell. We are now alone in the room, and Joe has a tear in his eye. He is used to making large and quick decisions in the business world, but this one is weighing on him.

At this moment, René calls. She wants to know the prognosis and the verdict.

"Hi, Joe, I am calling to check on you. Are you still in Lynnwood?"

"Yes, I am still here at the clinic. I am in the room with Bubba. The doctor and Jennifer just left. They did a paw pad pinch test on him." Joe explains to René the results of the test and the fact it establishes a neural connection from the bottom of his feet to his brain.

"Listen, I know I came up here today to put an end to his treatment, but I want to give him another week," Joe tells René.

"Honey, what changed your mind? We discussed this issue two weeks ago and gave it our best shot. Bubba hasn't moved or shown any signs of recovering. What makes you think another week will change anything?" René inquires.

"Everyone up here is working really hard on him, and the doctor mentioned it can take up to three weeks for him to show signs of recovery. If the doctor told me Bubba is not going to recover, then I can make the decision to put him down, but she is telling me another week may be needed. Look, you know how I feel about this dog. Go with me on this for one more week. If he doesn't show any sign of recovery, I will do what has to be done," Joe pleads with René.

"Joe, you have a hard time giving up on things. It is a good trait in you, but sometimes there are things you have to let go of because

61

it is for the best and it is the right thing to do. I will support you on this for one more week *if* you promise me you will do what is right and stick to your word on what you are telling me," René answers.

"Thanks, honey! I appreciate your support more than you know. I will be good with things if nothing changes during the week. I will be home soon. See you then." Joe signs off with René.

They're conversation ends, and now it is just the two of us again.

"Bubba, all these doctor-family conferences are draining the life out of me. I am doing all the heavy lifting. You have to give me some help here pretty soon," Joe says as he scratches my head. He opens the door and signals for Jennifer, asking her if she can get the doctor and come back to the room. All are in the room again.

Joe says, "My wife, family, and I really appreciate all that you have done for Bubba. We have discussed and decided to give Bubba a few more days, up to a week. However, if there is no marketable improvement by the end of the week, then I want you to put him down."

Later, I find out that this last-ditch effort by his daughter, Shawn, and Jennifer's impassioned plea are the main reasons Joe commits to the extra week. He doesn't think I will get any better; just simply out of loyalty to his family and the hard work and dedication of the technicians have won the day.

He leaves the clinic and sends a text message to René and Shawn: "We are keeping Bubba going for seven more days. Say a prayer for him."

Crescent Bar beach (wet)

Crescent Bar beach (front stance)

In front yard with ball and harness

Joe, Bengy and Bubba with ball in front yard

Bubba-front pyramid position

Bubba sitting up on a carpets on wooden floor

Bubba with red harness side view

4 BUBBA

Bubba, Bengy, Mac and Keely

Bubba swimming, returning stick-Crescent Bar

Young Bubba sitting on back of boat-duck hunting

Joe, Bubba and pheasants in front yard

Bubba in Montana

Rehab

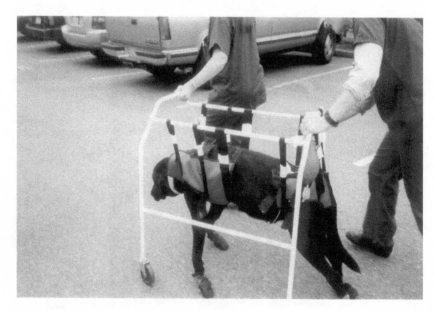

Rehab

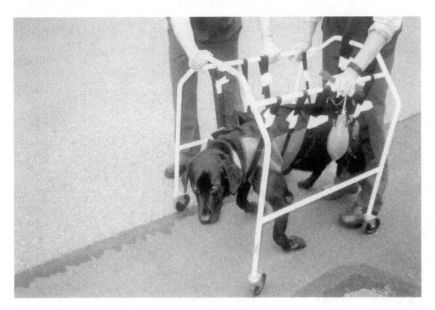

Rehab

Rehab

Bubba relaxing

Keely and Mac

CHAPTER **12**

First Movement!

A few days have gone by since the fourteen-day paw pad pinch test. Joe arrives for his daily visit. Little does he know I have a surprise in store. You see, dogs always like to wag their tails whenever we are happy, especially when we see someone we know. Since my neck injury, I haven't been able to do that, even though I am excited and happy to see someone come to visit me.

Today is going to be different. They have wheeled me into the visiting room on the stretcher, and I am anxiously waiting for Joe to arrive. Jennifer, the technician, is with me when the door opens and Joe walks in. As we glance upon each other, my tail wags back and forth, slapping the stretcher. A big, huge smile comes across his round face from ear to ear. He pats me on the head and asks Jennifer, "When did this happen?"

Jennifer tells him, "The technicians were massaging and stretching his limbs this morning, and he started to wag his tail."

It isn't much, but after all we have been through over the last two and half weeks, it is a start. It demonstrates that some level of healing is taking place inside my injured body.

The next day, Joe comes with Uncle Bob again. Bob has heard the news and wants to see me again. While they are here, besides wagging my tail, I move my right rear leg. They play with the paw on my rear right leg, and I attempt to pull it away and my leg moves.

Uncle Bob has sold me down the river over a week ago, but when he goes home and speaks to his wife, Kathy, tonight, he is going to have to tell her, "Bubba has a chance." Uncle Bob lets Joe know, if he can help get me back, he is volunteering.

René and Shawn come to visit the next day. René brings Keely to see me. She thinks this will give me motivation. Well, it does; I want to show Keely I can steal all the attention of René and Shawn even though she is here. While René and Shawn hover over me, patting me and talking to me, I give Keely a smile. Nice to see her, and she is gracious, letting me win the day attention-wise.

"Hi, Bubba! Your mommy has come to check on your progress and let you visit with Keely girl." René speaks softly while scratching between my ears.

I am so happy to see René and Shawn my tail wags from side to side.

"Mom, isn't it great Bubba has started to regain some movement? I wonder how long it will take for him to recover," Shawn says, talking out loud.

"Well, honey, according to your dad and the doctor, his recovery can take a while and it may only be partial. We have to stay positive in our thinking and hoping for his recovery but, at the same time, remain sober in the reality that his body can be too damaged to fully heal," René tells her daughter in order to keep her thinking grounded.

I am still a long way from walking again or having my legs support my body in a standing position, but it is a start. It has been twenty-four days since my injury, and Joe has another conference meeting with my doctor. Yesterday, on Joe's visit, I moved my right front leg, so besides being able to wag my tail, I have movement of both my legs on my right side.

"Good morning, Doc," Joe greets Dr. Johnson as she enters the room to join Jennifer and me.

"How are you doing? I guess it is nice to say we have some good news and progress to talk about regarding Bubba. Presently, Bubba has some movement of both his right legs, which demonstrates there is a level of healing taking place inside his body. Our original diagnosis was that his stroke was centered on his left side. The nonmovement of his left legs seems to prove that correct," the doctor responds.

"When do you think we can expect progress for his left side?" Joe asks.

"Let me ask you, now that we have movement returning to his body, what are your goals for Bubba?" the doctor inquires.

"Bubba will need to use all four limbs to support himself, go to the bathroom on his own, and walk in and out of the house under his own power. We have a flight of stairs in our house, but there is a door that can be closed to block the stairs if necessary. I know it's probably too much to expect to get my old dog back, that can run, jump, and hunt in the woods, but if he can just walk around the house, he can still be our family dog," Joe tells the doctor.

"As I said, it doesn't surprise me his left side is slower to respond. I would recommend that you view any progress to Bubba on a week-to-week basis. Each week, we should see more and more improvement in both his acquiring more movement to different parts of his body as well as his strength improving. If his recovery hits a plateau after a week, then it is a distinct possibility that this can be the limit of his recovery," the doctor discusses with Joe.

"Okay, I can approach his recovery and care on a week-to-week basis. What is the next step for him here?" Joe asks.

"I am going to order his urine catheter withdrawn. The technicians are building a four-wheel carriage to support Bubba's body weight in order to take him outside. We would like to wheel him outside a few times per day for the fresh air and bathroom breaks. Additionally, I will have his water solution and food supplement tube removed. We will attempt to feed him canned food and give him water from a bottle to drink. If necessary, we can give him an IV of water to keep him hydrated," the doctor continues as Jennifer, Joe, and I listen.

"I am also going to have the technicians work with him in moving from lying on his side to the pyramid position." Lying on the belly.

Joe is happy with the progress and, after discussions with my doctor, agrees to continue my treatment for another week. This is a positive meeting, but there is still a concern that it is a distinct possibility the FCE stroke to the left side of my neck has caused permanent paralysis to my left side.

An appointment is made for one week from now. Joe is now approaching my recovery treatment on a week-by-week basis, measuring progress and determining with my doctor if my recovery has hit a plateau.

CHAPTER 13

Pyramid Position and Four-Wheel Carriage

This week, rather than my lying on the side, they want me to hold the pyramid position. The pyramid position is where I have to lie on the floor on my belly, with my two front paws out in front of me, while holding my head up. A towel is looped under my jaw to help me hold my head up off the floor. I struggle to hold this position. My neck muscles are too weak and still partially paralyzed. It is hard for me to hold my head up. They place me in this position, but I keep flopping over on my left side. They rig up support pillows on one side, with the wall as support on my other side. They assist by holding me in this position. I tire very quickly trying to maintain the pyramid position.

In addition to working on the pyramid position, they work my legs, especially the left side. They pinch my paw pads every two hours when I am flipped to my other side and every six hours, when they stretch and exercise my legs. It is important for me to experience sensation in my left limbs.

The staff rigs up a four-wheel carriage to hold my body up off the ground while allowing my four legs to dangle down, barely touching the deck. It takes four technicians to hook me up in this carriage and wheel me outside of the clinic. They put four leather boots on all four of my paw pads. These leather boots protect my paws from scraping the ground as they drag along when the technicians push the carriage. I have lost all muscle memory on how to move my legs in a walking motion. It is nice to smell the fresh air again, though.

Toward the end of this week's long period, Joe comes for his weekly doctor conference. I am able to hold the pyramid position for a short time without the support of the pillows or the wall and the towel looped under my jaw.

I am starting to twitch my rear left paw. The movement is more of a minor reflex action, but it is movement. The movement in both of my right legs is more pronounced and stronger. Everyone is pleased with the progress I am making this week. I am not up standing or walking yet, but I haven't hit a plateau with my recovery either. My body is still healing, even if slowly.

I have been in the Last Chance Dog Hotel about five weeks, and so far, I have gone from being completely paralyzed to wagging my tail, moving my right legs, and twitching my rear left leg. The next step is to ascertain movement to my front left leg and be able to rise up and hold a standing position. In order to attempt this maneuver, the technicians have to support my body weight around my midsection with two towels. They run one towel underneath my chest right in the back of my two front legs and another towel under my belly, right in front of my two back legs. My body weight is down to ninety-two pounds. I have lost thirty-three pounds since the injury and my arrival here.

The technicians pull up on the towels to lift me up, but my legs just kind of dangle, unable to support my body. As they release any pressure off the towels, thus letting my body weight go to my legs, I immediately sprawl back to the floor. The weight of my body is just too heavy for my weak, semiparalyzed legs.

Joe walks into the room while Jennifer and a few of the technicians are trying to get me to stand.

"Hi, Jennifer! Hey, everybody. How is Bubba doing today?" he asks.

"Well, we are lifting him into a standing position by pulling up on the towels then slowly releasing support of the towels, transferring some of his weight to his legs," the technician explains.

"Has he been able to stand on his own, even for a moment?" Joe inquires.

"No. His legs are too weak, or he just does not have enough control over them yet. His left side is still mostly paralyzed," Jennifer chimes in.

"Let us try this. I have a dog treat with me. This time, when you lift him, I will hold the dog treat slightly above his nose, making him have to reach up to get it. It may motivate him to momentarily stand," Joe says, thinking out loud with the technicians.

This time, when the technicians lift me, I catch a scent of a dog treat in Joe's hand. Immediately, my attention focuses on Joe's right hand. As the technicians start to release the support from the towels looped around my body, Joe opens his right hand with the dog treat in it.

"Hey, Bubba, you want this dog treat?" Joe says while holding the dog treat slightly above my nose.

I raise my head up while stiffening my two right legs and snatch the dog treat from his hand.

"Nice job, Bubba," Joe congratulates me while the technicians all smile at this small accomplishment.

"He hesitated momentarily after we released the support off the two towels," Jennifer states.

"It is a moment today, but if we all continue to work at it with him, it can be a minute tomorrow or next week. We need to appreciate these small improvements and try to build on them. I am very impressed by all of you working so diligently with Bubba," Joe states to the technicians.

CHAPTER 14

Four Corners

I cannot get up, sit up, or stand up. I have movement to my right legs and minor movement to my left back leg. Food motivates me, and seeing that I have lost thirty pounds since being here, even more now. Joe and sissy, Shawn, show up from their lunch break, and if my nose serves me correctly, and it usually does, I smell hamburgers. They have smuggled hamburgers into the clinic even though I am on a strict doctor-prescribed diet.

We are in a private room with a linoleum floor, much too slippery for me to move on, but Joe has a carpet brought in and rolled out onto the floor of the room. They place me on the center of the carpet. I can smell those hamburgers—must be either in Shawn's purse or Joe's jacket pocket. They have a new game called four corners. It comes from basketball, when one team is trying to run out the clock on the other team. They spread out four players and pass the ball around in order to stall while running out the clock.

Their idea of four corners today is to break off a piece of the hamburger and place it on the corner of the carpet farthest from my nose, whereby I have to spin and move my body to get it. I scratch and claw my nails into the carpet in an attempt to drag my body to the corner of the carpet where the piece of hamburger is located. To accomplish this, it is necessary for me to flex every muscle in my body that I have control over. It is exhausting, but finally, I get the piece of hamburger. Then Joe puts another piece of hamburger at the complete opposite end of the carpet, and I start all over again.

Why doesn't he just feed me the hamburger? Can't he see that I am really struggling just for a small piece of food to eat? I question myself.

The exercise is forcing me to really flex the muscles I have limited, partial control over in order to drag my body sideways across the carpet. I flip over from side to side in the process, depending on where Joe places the hamburger. Utterly exhausted, I play the game because I like the food and this exercise is helping me regain the use of my muscles.

It is kind of like doing an isometric. Just to flip from my side to the pyramid position without help is strenuous for me. It also forces me to use my neck muscles to hold my head up whenever I find myself on my belly. Then at the end of the exercise, with the last piece of hamburger, Joe places this piece on the edge of the seat of the chair. If I want it, I am going to have to rise up partially to get it. I raise my head as far as it will go and try to snatch the piece of hamburger with my tongue, but it is too high. Joe stands over me and assists by raising my body slightly up with his hands; he wants me to work at it and yet help too. I am exhausted, but I exert all my energy and finally snatch the food from the seat.

Somehow, I know this little lunch visit is not part of the doctor's orders, but Joe and Shawn play this often with me from now on. It is a tremendous amount of work for a little bit of good-tasting food, but I enjoy the game and the pleasure of their company.

When Shawn comes and plays four corners with me, I can get her to give me pieces of the hamburger if I moan and cry, as she has a soft spot in her heart for me.

CHAPTER 15

Swimming Again

It is early August. The weather is nice, and the water of Lake Washington is about as warm as it gets. The doctor and Joe discuss if my body is still too heavy for my weak legs, then why not make my body buoyant in the water and see if I remember how to swim? I have always been a strong swimmer.

Joe goes to a boat supply store and buys a dog floatation device for my body. Uncle Bob and Joe arrive at lunchtime in the pickup truck. I am loaded into the back of the truck with instructions from the doctor not to overdo it. It feels good to be leaving the Last Chance Dog Hotel, even if it is going to be for a few hours. We arrive at Denny Creek Beach Park in Kirkland, Washington, on the shores of Lake Washington. Familiar smells of this location fill my senses. Memories of Mommy René bringing me here on numerous occasions in the past come flooding back. She would throw a ball in the water, allowing me to swim and fetch it. In my exuberance, I would run down the beach in front of the bulkhead wall crashing into waves, getting wet. I love this place and have many great memories coming here with René while my master was away at work.

"Hey, Bubba, you remember this place?" Joe hollers.

"Woof!" I attempt to bark as we pull into the parking lot. Due to the paralysis to my neck, I've lost the ability to give a full bark, but lately, it is coming back.

How am I going to get to the water from the truck? I think.

"Hey, Bob, can you grab the large Mexican serape blanket from the back seat?" Joe asks Bob.

"Sure. Is it our stretcher to carry Bubba to the lake in?" Bob inquires.

I am dying to get into the water. Can't these two move any faster? I patiently wait as Bob and Joe lay out the blanket.

"All right, you grab two corners, and I will grab two corners and haul him to the edge of the lake. Once there, I will need to put this dog life jacket on him I bought at the boat store," Joe says.

It is a beautiful, sunshine, blue-sky day with a slight breeze. The water is very calm. All of a sudden, Joe pulls out a decoy duck.

Oh, man, my weakness! My body jitters with excitement.

I have on my new life jacket, and into the water go Uncle Bob, Joe, and I until the water is deep enough for me to float. Joe throws the decoy duck about twenty-five feet from me into the lake. I focus on the duck and start moving—well, more like flailing my two right legs while kicking my left back leg. I am completely buoyant with the life preserver on, making slow progress toward the duck. With all my might, I softly caress the decoy duck. With it secure in my mouth, I turn right (left is not an option anymore) and begin swimming slowly back to Uncle Bob and Joe. They are more thrilled than I am. Both are cheering me on while standing in frigid water just above their knees.

This is what I live for! *Oh, boy! Oh, boy!* I fetch the decoy duck four or five times. I am breathing heavily, tired, but having one heck of a good time. I feel like a regular dog again. Now, mind you, I wasn't actually swimming like I used to, more like just thrashing around, the main function coming from my right legs, with an occasional kick from my back left. If it weren't for the life jacket, my ability to propel my body above the water would have been impossible. The important thing, I am free and under my own power, without someone having to carry me. You see, to massage or exercise my legs while I lie on the floor only takes one technician. It takes four technicians to go outside of the vet clinic in the four-wheel carriage or to do the standing exercise with the two towels. This is real freedom again.

I hear Uncle Bob and Joe talking, saying, "Would you have thought just a couple of weeks ago we would be out here doing this with this dog? Why, I almost buried old Bubba on three different occasions!"

Uncle Bob and Joe get me to stand in the shallow water. The water is up to the middle of my body, making me light and buoyant. I don't want to leave, but the doctor has given Joe strict orders to not overdo it. Uncle Bob and Joe wrap me back up in the Mexican serape blanket and carry me back up to the truck. They have to go back to work, and I have to go back to the Last Chance Dog Hotel.

I found out later that Uncle Bob told his wife, Kathy, "Maybe Bubba has a chance after all."

Today, being out in the fresh air, away from the clinic, and swimming in the lake has been fun.

The next day, the technicians try to work with me to go from the pyramid position to the standing position, but I am worn-out and sore from the previous day's adventure to the lake. My body feels like a soft, wet noodle. I want to sleep and rest. They massage and stretch my legs. My muscle tone is good, and no atrophy has set into any of my legs, including my left front leg, which still hasn't moved yet. By the end of the fifth week, actually closer to forty days since the injury, I begin to move my front left leg.

The swimming trips to the lake and when four technicians have time to hook me up into the four-wheel carriage and take me outside to the parking lot of the clinic give me the opportunity to be outdoors again. Even though I have to be strapped into this homemade contraption with belts and have Velcro boots for my paws, it gives me a chance to relieve myself outside like a regular dog again. They always stop under a tree and just let me smell the surroundings. I can't tell you how many times these technicians have had to clean me up over the last five weeks. Life is better, but I need to learn how to walk again.

CHAPTER 16

Eviction Notice

Joe arrives at the clinic to discuss my current progress and situation with the doctor. While lying on the floor, I listen intently as they discuss my recovery and transition to rehabilitation. The doctor explains to Joe that their facility is not set up to do rehabilitation. They are an emergency facility to attend to injury and trauma into recovery. Once recovery has begun, they usually send the pet home with care instructions or back to the vet clinic that originally referred the pet. Any rehabilitation is between the pet owner, pet, and rehab facility. They need Joe to make arrangements for me to receive rehab and leave their clinic. Medically, there is nothing further the Lynnwood vet clinic can do for me. Whether I survive and walk again will depend on the quality of rehab I receive.

"Good morning, Joe. We need to discuss with you the rehabilitation of Bubba, which will ultimately determine if he is ever going to walk again. Our facility is an emergency care center to treat trauma. Once we have treated and arrested the injury of the animal, we then refer the pet back to the local pet clinic. In your case, Bubba requires long-term rehab therapy," Dr. Johnson explains to Joe.

"Bubba can't walk or stand on his own. I can't take him home in this condition," he pleads with Dr. Johnson.

"Yes, that is correct. However, if he is to learn how to walk again, you must find a rehab facility. We are not set up or staffed to teach him to walk again. We are exercising his legs and stretching his muscles, which has prevented muscle atrophy, but now that he is beginning to move his limbs, he needs rehab therapy to learn to walk," the doctor explains.

This presents a problem to Joe, because I still can't walk and he has promised René he will not bring me home until I can walk on my own. Remember, it took four technicians just to take me outside in the carriage. Many dogs that experience FCE may only have it affect one or two limbs with partial paralysis. They can go home in two to three weeks, fumble around, and walk unassisted in the yard. They can relieve themselves and perform their normal bodily functions. However, my FCE is an acute full paralysis to all four of my legs. It has been over six weeks, and although my progress hasn't hit a plateau, my healing and recovery is slow. One has to consider that it may be a reality that I will never be able to walk again under my own power. Before Joe leaves, Jennifer talks to him and gives him a copy of a brochure regarding rehab services from a clinic in Redmond, Washington, and Ballard, Washington.

"Joe, I know you are getting pressured to find a rehab facility. I am not allowed to do this, but here are a few brochures on canine rehab facilities," Jennifer explains while handing Joe two brochures.

"What do you know about these facilities?" he asks.

"Really not too much. This has never happened before with another dog. I can get in serious trouble for recommending a specific facility to you. You need to do your own research and homework then choose the one you think will be best to help Bubba," Jennifer tells him.

"Can you please put those brochures in your pocket so I don't get into any trouble?" Jennifer reiterates.

"Listen, Jennifer, you have been really helpful throughout this whole ordeal. *Mum's* the word." Joe winks at her.

Joe checks out both thoroughly, but neither will be able to long-term board me while I am being rehabilitated. He also discovers a facility in Central Oregon some 250 miles away that advertises rehab therapy and long-term boarding. He goes home and discusses all these options with René and the costs associated with each. Again, it seems my family, my support system, are at a crossroads as to how to proceed and if proceeding is a viable option. Currently, all medical costs have now totaled $5,700 since I first collapsed on the front lawn. Now we are talking about finding an intensive rehab program that can also board me. Sending me to Oregon is too far away. With having my family close by, the daily visits keep all members in touch with my progress and condition. René has a serious conversation with Joe regarding how much more we can afford to spend on a dog that may never be able to walk again. Why, I can't even stand up on my own.

"Joe, I can't see bringing Bubba all the way to Oregon for rehab. It will take seven hours to drive one way just to see him. You need to figure out a solution for him here, where we can stay in touch," René opines.

"Well, the two that offer rehab therapy don't long-term board. One is here in Redmond, and the other all the way over in Ballard. The one in Redmond is more just water therapy in a pool. The one in Ballard sounds more high-tech. It is called water hydrotherapy," Joe responds.

"Listen, you need to check them both out and honestly decide if either of them can really help Bubba walk again. I know he has progressed, but he is not close to walking or even standing on his own. See which one of these clinics has had past successes with canine FCE and get them to give you an honest assessment of Bubba's chances. I know this is emotional for you, as it is for all of us, but you promised you would stay grounded and be logical throughout this process. Realistically, how much longer and how much more money are we to spend on a dog we all love but may never walk again?" René logically talks to Joe, trying to keep him focused on this important next step.

Joe scratches Oregon off the list, researches the two local rehab clinics, and plans to meet with them to get a realistic prognosis of my future. He has not realized how much he has spent so far because he has compartmentalized my situation into weekly progress. Even though I make weekly progress, he has not projected forward the number of weeks it may take, if ever, for me to be rehabilitated. Between Lynnwood giving Joe notice that he needs to move on and

René's summarizing my current costs, Joe finds himself at a decision point again.

Joe chooses the rehab clinic in Ballard to examine me and discuss my chances. He needs an accurate future projection of my health respective to costs.

CHAPTER 17

Water Hydrotherapy

In Ballard, about fifteen miles from Joe's work and the Lynnwood clinic, is Sunrise Vet run by Dr. Alene Lamp. Let me describe Dr. Lamp and her clinic.

Dr. Lamp received her bachelor of arts in English literature from Colby College. She then attended Harvard, where she completed all the prerequisite coursework for veterinary school. She moved from Boston to the Pacific Northwest to attend Washington State University's College of Veterinary Medicine. Dr. Lamp received her doctorate of veterinary medicine in 2000 and moved to Seattle to begin her career in small-animal medicine.

As her career in veterinary medicine progressed, she realized that there was a lack of physical rehabilitation for canines like me. She completed a certificate program from the Canine Rehabilitation Institute in 2005 to become a certified canine rehabilitation therapist, the first one to practice in Seattle. This was to be really lucky for me.

Thus, she opened Sunrise Vet and Rehab Center to combine the two professions she adored: general veterinary practice and physical rehabilitation. I was being referred to Dr. Lamp, and the fate of my future was going to rest with her.

This is my first visit to meet Dr. Lamp. Joe and I arrive in his truck. Dr. Lamp and one of her technicians, Jen, come out to meet us. They strap me onto a stretcher and carry me inside to an examination room. I am examined to determine the amount of feeling and sensation that I have in my limbs as well as my muscle tone and if any muscle atrophy has developed.

I hear Joe talking with Dr. Lamp regarding my condition and chances. Joe explains to her, in order to bring me home, I need to regain the ability to walk on my own. Our house has a level of steep stairs. Additionally, things are getting quite busy as his only daughter, Shawn Nichol, is getting married in less than a month.

Between Joe working in Los Angeles and Seattle and the family planning for a big wedding, there is no room for a large paralyzed dog at the house. He needs an honest diagnosis of my condition, with a real estimate as to my ability to be physically rehabilitated.

Dr. Lamp levels with Joe and lets him know that my condition is extreme; however, I have good muscle tone and good reflection when my limbs are stretched out. She wants to work with me for two to three times per week, performing her new hydrotherapy. Dr. Lamp has a large glass tank that measures eight feet long, three feet wide, and five feet deep, with a treadmill on the bottom of the tank. This glass tank has a door at one end in order to gain entrance. Once closed, the glass tank is watertight. I am carried into the tank and laid on the floor—actually, the treadmill. The door is closed tight. Dr. Lamp, Jen, and I are in the tank together. All of a sudden, the tank quickly starts filling with warm, eighty-eight-degree-temperature chlorinated water. The idea is to immerse me into the water to allow my body to become buoyant. Just like swimming in the lake, this buoyancy decreases the pressure on my joints. The heated water increases blood circulation to any inflamed joints. This type of therapy has been used on people for years, but this is the first time it's been available for canines.

Even though I am more buoyant in the water, without the life jacket on, I am unable to stand, and due to my weakened, paralyzed neck muscles, I struggle to keep my head above the water. Dr. Lamp is unable to start the treadmill unless I can at least stand up. Joe tells Dr. Lamp he has a dog life jacket in his truck, and she directs him to bring it in. Once I have the life jacket on and a little more water is added to the tank, I am buoyant enough to stand up.

As soon as the treadmill starts, my legs fold under me and I slide to the rear of the tank into Jen's arms. Dr. Lamp stops the treadmill and has the idea that if Joe can support my body by holding onto the handle of the life jacket from above, thus steadying me, she can move my front legs and Jen can move my rear legs all in a simulated walking motion on the treadmill while under the water.

We are a sight to see, Dr. Lamp and Jen immerse in full blue medical clothing in the water tank, moving my legs in a coordinated dog-walking motion, while Joe is holding me up from on top by holding on to the handle of my life jacket. The treadmill is moving beneath us. I can feel my legs walking under me, but it isn't as if all the commands are coming from my brain. I am now on the road to re-establishing some lost muscle memory that I am going to need if I am going to learn how to walk again.

We perform this walking exercise on the treadmill in the water tank three times for two minutes each time. I am exhausted after the third time. The water is quickly drained from the tank, and I am carried out to the shower tub, washed off, and dried. Afterward, Dr. Lamp discusses with Joe what expectations should be for me.

"Bubba has the most acute case of canine FCE to his whole body I have ever come into contact with. Reviewing his records and speaking with Dr. Johnson, I understand his paralysis was complete from the neck down. We have never rehabbed a totally paralyzed dog before. However, he is young and has great muscle tone. Lynnwood has done an outstanding job keeping his reflection while fighting off muscle atrophy."

Joe inquires, "Dr. Lamp, I need to know realistically what Bubba's chances are for him to walk again under his own power. Please don't give me any pie-in-the-sky chances or prognosis. My wife and I have been going back and forth on Bubba's treatment over the past six-plus weeks. I need to be able to go home and give her a fair assessment of what the future holds if you treat Bubba."

"First off, we don't give pie-in-the-sky prognosis here at Sunrise. I will be straightforward with you regarding his treatment. I project we can have Bubba walking again within thirty days. It is going to resemble a wobbly, drunk type of walk at first. It will get better over time, but I will need some time and additional water therapy workouts to revise and better assess him," Dr. Lamp reports to Joe.

"What about the differences between his left versus his right side?" Joe asks.

"I concur with Lynnwood. His left side is more affected by the stroke, especially his left front paw. There is no atrophy in his left paw, but he seems to want to keep it curled, with the paw pad facing up, instead of placing it with the paw pad facing the floor. Two things are possible, and only time will tell for sure. His left side may only recover partially and achieve less-regular movement than his right side, or over time, his left side may eventually recover equally to his right. It will just take longer to do so. Therapy and time will determine his recovery. The good news is that you are bringing to me a healthy young dog to work with. Once muscle atrophy sets in, we cannot reverse the process. Bubba has no atrophy," she states with confidence.

Joe signs me up for ten water-tank hydrotherapy treatments (two per week). Additionally, Dr. Lamp feels the swimming in Lake Washington can be continued. It will be good cross-training therapy; however, I need to rest the day before hydrotherapy.

Joe takes me back to Lynnwood and discusses with my doctor his plans for my rehabilitation. He needs to continue my boarding at Lynnwood until my rehab therapy starts to kick in and gets me ambulatory. Lynnwood reiterates their position about finding me other boarding or taking me home, but Joe negotiates two more weeks from them and they agree. Joe and Dr. Lamp draw up a Bubba schedule that includes swimming in Lake Washington and water hydrotherapy at Ballard over the ensuing weeks. Now Joe goes home to tell René that I should be walking in just a few weeks and we will need to come up with a plan and a place to keep me at the house. Joe knows this is potentially an optimistic outlook for me; however, he is getting squeezed from the need to find me other boarding, the ongoing costs of treatment, work, and the events swirling around the

Flynn household. He needs to do some serious convincing to René that there is still hope for me and the financial investment is worth it.

The additional treatment in Ballard, coupled with my stay in Lynnwood, is going to move my weekly cost to $1,000 per week. Joe is the one most involved with my treatment and visits, as René has her hands full planning a wedding, running a household, and caring for Keely. René wants to know how, all of a sudden, I will be walking in two weeks, ready to come home. She is surprised Joe has agreed to the future treatments and potential move home for me without first discussing it. How is she going to care for a large handicapped dog? Is Joe going to stop traveling? Cut back his work schedule? These are good questions, and definitely a voice of reason. You see, I am still a long shot, and the cost of maintaining me is getting higher each week.

In addition to everything going on, they are worried about their son, Dan, in Iraq, who is due to come home for the wedding. However, he hasn't called or emailed in three weeks. They have the cost and preparation of Shawn and Brent's wedding, which is going to be fifty more guests than what has originally been planned. Joe is struggling with his job, as the company's financing and capital were pulled shortly after my stroke. With my master as the main financial provider for the family, this leaves him stressed with work, and it demands more of his time at the office and work-related travel.

I know this story is about me and the struggle I am going through; however, my family support system is being stretched at the seams. This support system needs to stay united between my family members, rehab facility, and boarding facility if I am going to make it.

René disagrees with Joe about bringing me home in two weeks. This is the first break in my support system.

"Joe, how could you commit to another month of therapy before we had a chance to discuss it first?" René asks Joe.

"Listen, I am the point man on Bubba like you are the point person on Shawn's wedding. I am relying on you to make good decisions for us regarding the wedding, as you should be on me making good decisions regarding Bubba," Joe states defensively in a strong tone.

"We discussed a budget for the wedding together, and whenever a change comes up, I have brought that to your attention before committing to anything. Do you see the difference?" René responds inquiringly.

"Yes, the difference is a wedding can be planned, and families have a general idea what to expect. We are in uncharted waters here with Bubba. It is astounding we have even gotten this far. Now he has a realistic shot with this rehab clinic and Dr. Lamp. Is it going to cost more money and take more time? Yes, but I think he is worth it. We have come too far not to keep going. Don't ask me to back off now," Joe finishes as he walks into the other room with his back to René.

"I can see the difference clearly. I discuss things with you and you make decisions regarding Bubba in a vacuum by yourself. Why are you walking away from me?" She follows him to the other room. "Just because a new doctor tells you she can get him to walk in two weeks on experimental-type treatment . . . I expect you to discuss it with me before making a go-ahead commitment. The costs are mounting on his care, and he is still a very paralyzed dog that you can't bring home if he is not walking!" René finishes.

"Well, if Bubba can't come home, maybe I won't be here either." Joe walks out the front door and decides to rent a hotel room.

René tries to speak to him, but he packs a small suitcase and leaves.

Pizza Box

Between a few more swim trips to Lake Washington with Uncle Bob and Joe and a couple more hydrotherapy sessions with Dr. Lamp, I am gaining strength and more movement to my limbs. So much so that I am actually able to do a commando-type crawl around the linoleum floor of the operating room at the Lynnwood vet clinic.

One evening, the staff is busy with three new arriving clients. All three dogs require emergency surgery. You see, the staff is used to me just lying on my pee blanket off to the side of the floor, so it is rewarding for them to see me slowly crawling around to say hello to them.

Tonight, I have an ulterior motive. Right before the three dogs came in, the staff was in the middle of eating pizza in the break room. Now they are all feverishly working to save and repair the three dogs when I zero in on the smell and aroma of cheese, pepperoni, and sausage coming from the break room, which is located on the far side of the operating room. Slowly I start my crawl around the side of the operating room floor toward the unattended pizza in the break room. I keep my focus on the pizza scent as if I were out in the field, hunting pheasant again. Although the staff has eaten most of the pizza, I spot a pizza box on the floor of the break room smothered in flavor and containing many pieces of uneaten crust. My commando crawl is basically me in the pyramid position, gripping my nail claws into the floor, dragging myself. I finally arrive in the break room at the pizza box. Upon devouring all the pizza crust inside the box, I begin to eat the actual pizza box. You see, it is covered in flavor and pasta grease. I am just about done when one of the technicians discovers me. He is wondering where the box has gone, but upon his seeing I have a piece of it in my mouth, I am busted.

They have to find a new place to put me in the clinic because, with my commando crawl, I have become an ambulatory patient. No longer can they just let me lie on the floor. They have a new area for me off in another room. They can see me, but the entrance is blocked off with carts and boxes.

On Joe's next visit, the doctor makes a point of it to inform Joe that my days are numbered at the clinic; he needs to have me moved.

CHAPTER 19

Support Team Breaking Apart!

Joe and René are not in agreement in support of my continued rehab therapy, and to complicate matters more, Joe has to fly to Denver, Colorado, to tend to his parents. Joe spent one night in the hotel after his last disagreement with René and went home, and they didn't speak for a few days, then he headed off to Denver. His parents are in their mideighties and suffering from Alzheimer's disease. Joe has moved his parents from New Jersey to Denver the year before to be closer to him and his brother, Tom. His brother called regarding taking the car keys away from his dad so that he can't drive anymore. They are wandering off and getting lost, so it is important for them to discuss a change in their care situation. Joe holds power of attorney with regard to his parents' welfare.

I am glad Joe is going to Denver, because his parents are much more important than me; however, I am at a critical junction, and the loss of my star player and supporter can't come at a worst time. Joe's brother, Tom, meets him at the Denver airport so they can discuss a strategy.

"Hey, Tom, thanks for picking me up. It is good to see you," Joe says.

"Well, it is good to have you here. We have to get something done with Mom and Dad before something bad happens to them," Tom tells his brother.

"Come on, it can't be that bad. I just visited four months ago, and things seemed pretty stable then," Joe answers.

"Dad is just driving off in the car, thinking he can drive to Brooklyn, New York. He thinks he is only fifteen to twenty minutes away. He ends up getting lost, and strangers call me to go pick him up," Tom says.

"When did this start happening?" Joe inquires.

"Remember when I called you about a month ago? I left you a message to come down for a visit," Tom states.

"Yes, but you didn't say anything like this was going on," Joe responds.

"Things started about that time. In the middle of the night, Dad would pack the car up with everything he could stuff into it, and in the morning, I would talk to him and we would unpack it. Then a few nights would go by and he would pack it up again. I know you are busy with your job, your daughter is getting married, and your dog is in trouble, so I figured you have your hands full. I have been trying to handle things, but now something has to change," Tom says, opening up to Joe.

"Anything else I need to know?" Joe asks.

"Most of the time, Dad thinks I am his brother, Hughie, instead of his son. Sometimes he doesn't know who Mom is. He will ask me, 'Who is that lady living here?'" Tom tells his stunned brother.

"Wow, I knew Mom's Alzheimer's was bad, but I thought Dad's would take a while to catch up. It seems his is advancing more rapidly than Mom's now," Joe states his opinion and continues. "Is Dad open to us discussing a move with him and Mom into a care facility?"

"Listen, I tried to discuss it with him, and he just about threw me out of their place. You can try while you are here, but I don't think it will do much good. Remember how hard it was and how long it took you just to get them to move out here from New Jersey last year?" Tom reminds his brother. "The other problem is, not any facility will take them. They need a facility that will limit coming and going. They need to be watched. If they don't go willingly, which I know they won't, we are going to need to have them committed. That takes time," Tom continues to explain.

"Tom, this couldn't come at a worse time for me. My job is pulling me in ten different directions. I have some tough choices I am facing there. René is handling the wedding, and that all seems to be fine, but this tragedy with Bubba is starting to pull us apart," Joe says, opening up to his brother.

"Joe, is the dog savable?" Tom asks.

"I don't know. It has been a long, slow road so far. René thinks I should have my head examined, and at times, I think she is right. Something has got to give here pretty soon. Let's go see Mom and Dad right now so I can see for myself," Joe answers his brother.

They leave the airport and drive to their parents' two-bedroom condo, which is located on a golf course. They spend the better part of the day together, visiting and going to look at senior retirement care facilities. Joe's dad wants nothing to do with any care facility. He calls them all loony bins.

Later that night, Joe and his brother, Tom, go off together to come up with a plan.

"What do you think of me moving out of my place, putting my stuff in storage, and moving in with Mom and Pop for the time being?" Tom asks his brother.

"I think that would be great, if you are willing to do it. It will at least handle the temporary situation we have with them. I think we need to still take Dad's car keys away from him," Joe tells his brother.

"I tried that several times. He gets really upset if you even bring it up," Tom responds.

"How about I just take the car and drive it over to your son's house in Longmont and leave it there? We can tell Dad it is stolen and we are searching for it," Joe says, thinking out loud.

"Okay with me. It is your plan, so I will let you break the news to him tomorrow morning about it being stolen over breakfast." Tom pokes at his brother.

"Fine with me. Let's go," Joe responds.

The next morning, Joe arrives for breakfast at his parents' apartment. His brother, Tom, is in the kitchen, cooking bacon and eggs. Coffee is already brewed and hot. As Joe enters the apartment, he notices that his father is outfitted in his dress A uniform from the US Army.

"Well, good morning. How is everybody this morning? Dad, what's up with the full-dress army uniform this morning?" Joe inquires after greeting his mom and dad.

"They want me to report into my old outfit at Fort Dix, New Jersey," his dad answers.

Joe looks over at his brother while he walks to the other side of the dining table and gives his mom a kiss on the top of the head. Joe's mom's Alzheimer's has progressed to a point where she does not really acknowledge directly a specific person's presence. However, she does seem to know that she is around family.

"Dad, you are retired from the army. That's why they send you a check every month. You need to stay here with us and Mom," Joe reminds his dad.

"What do you mean? I am not retired yet!" his dad tells his son while giving him a big smile.

Joe reaches over to the framed certificate of retirement hanging on the wall and lays it on the table. "Let's read this together, Dad. It says here you served over twenty years of honorable service to your country, and we are all very proud of you for it."

"So they don't want me to show up at Fort Dix?" his dad asks.

"No, Dad, they want you to be here with us and Mom. We need you to be here, helping us watch over Mom." Joe speaks softly to his dad.

"Okay, who is ready for some bacon and eggs?" Tom asks from the kitchen.

"Hey, Dad, what do you think of this ex-Air Force guy making us breakfast? It sure smells good." Joe rips his brother. Their dad likes the thick army bacon.

"Oh, he does a good job whenever he comes over," Joe's father says, trying to credit his other son. "Should I change out of my uniform before we eat?"

"No, Dad, you look outstanding in it, and it kind of makes me extra proud to sit here and enjoy breakfast with you. You know your grandson Dan is wearing that same uniform, and he is over in Iraq, serving for us right now. He will be proud, too, to be able to sit here and have breakfast with you," Joe says to his father.

"Hey, brother, food's hot, coffee is hot, let's eat." Joe's brother, Tom, brings the hot plates to the table. The two brothers and their parents enjoy a family breakfast together.

Joe's trip to Denver ends with his parents' car being parked at his nephew's house. His brother, Tom, moves in with his parents in order to keep an eye on them. This is a workable solution to care for his parents as they both progress into the later stages of Alzheimer's. It is also a generous sacrifice on the part of his brother, as he leaves the college he is teaching at.

Right before Joe left for Denver, Uncle Bob and Joe took me for a swim trip to Lake Washington and really worked me hard. Joe talked to the technicians in Lynnwood, instructing them to take me outside in the four-wheel carriage three times per day plus work me with the two towels, doing the stand-up exercise from the prone position twice per day. Shawn shuttled me down to Ballard for a hydrotherapy session. Joe felt that if we could put a full-court press onto all aspects of my rehab therapy, he could excel my progress, even though doctor's orders were to not overdo it. Joe was working against the deadline of having to move me out of the Lynnwood facility and the need for me to get up and walk so he could bring me home.

My next hydrotherapy session is scheduled. Joe is in Denver, and Shawn has to leave town on a business work trip. Joe calls René from Denver to have her take me to this next session. He knows it is important that I not miss a session and thinks it will be good for René to see firsthand the progress I am making through hydro-therapy. What he doesn't know is that I am worn-out from all the cross-training and in need of rest.

René drives the truck up to Lynnwood from Redmond in the pouring rain. Upon her arrival, the Lynnwood clinic has emergencies in their operating room, causing a ninety-minute delay in loading me in the truck for my trip to Ballard. Upon my arrival in Ballard at Sunrise Vet, René and Jen put me on their stretcher and bring me into the clinic. They massage my limbs to get me ready for the water tank. This is René's first time to see me perform in hydrotherapy.

Dr. Lamp and Jen are in the tank with me as René curiously looks on with anticipation. The treadmill starts and, my legs fold under me as I slide into Jen's arms at the rear of the tank. Dr. Lamp has attempted the exercise two more times when she comes to the realization that I am an exhausted dog.

René looks on and sees a crippled dog that looks like he is getting worse since the last time she saw me ten days ago. Dr. Lamp tells René that I have performed much better in my other visits; however, nothing can change the visual picture of defeat I have painted in René's mind with my tragic performance. She is thinking, *Joe needs to have his head examined if he thinks Bubba will be well enough to bring home in a week or so.*

They package me up onto the stretcher; however, to top things off, a furniture truck is parked in the loading zone. René and Jen have to carry me half a block to his truck in the down-pouring rain. It is late, and due to the rain, the freeway is a parking lot. It takes two and a half hours for René to drive me back to Lynnwood and then for her to drive home to Redmond from Lynnwood. Upon our arrival back at Lynnwood, it is still pouring down rain and the clinic is still in emergency mode from their earlier operations. They can't spare anyone to come out to assist with moving me back inside for a good forty-five minutes. While René waits in the front sitting room area, the administrative manager comes to ask her some questions.

"We called Joe earlier today with regard to him moving Bubba home by the end of this week. Can you confirm with us which day he plans on doing that?"

René simmers while explaining to her that her husband is handling the decisions relating to me and that she will ask him to call her. Finally, they load me inside and René heads home. She leaves Redmond at ten o'clock in the morning and is getting in soaking wet after six o'clock at night.

Joe calls later that night from Denver to see how the day went.

"Hi, honey, it's me. I have been out with my parents and brother most of the day. We went to look at a few possible places for them to move to. It didn't go too well, as my parents are very close-minded toward moving to any type of senior care facility. To compound matters, not just any facility will take them because both are suffering from different degrees of Alzheimer's disease," Joe says, starting off the conversation. "How did things go with you and Bubba today? What did you think of the water hydrotherapy?" Joe asks excitedly. Joe is on thin ice, and he knows it!

"Maybe it would be best if we discussed Bubba's day when you come home. I don't want to add more things to your plate for you to worry about. It wasn't a good day for him, and it was a long day for me. However, you need to concentrate on your parents. We can deal with Bubba when you come home and have more time." René is trying to console him, keeping the focus on Joe's parents.

"Come on, I could use some good news on his progress. Give me something," Joe probes.

"Well, Joe, Bubba is still a very crippled dog. Dr. Lamp thought he might have been too exhausted from all the things you have him doing. He literally collapsed in the water tank when she turned on the treadmill," René answers.

Joe sits on the other end of the line in silence for a few moments. Then he says, "Listen, thanks for taking him over to Ballard. I know with traffic from the east side to Lynnwood then Ballard and back again, it can be hectic. I will call Dr. Lamp in the morning."

"Joe, it is important that you and your brother get things settled with your parents while you are there. We can discuss Bubba later, okay?" she responds.

"Sure, listen, my brother is coming. I need to run," he answers.

"Okay, call me back when you can."

The conversation ends.

In the morning, before flying out from Denver back to Seattle, Joe calls Dr. Lamp to discuss the previous day's events. She questions Joe as to how much other activity he has me doing besides water therapy. Joe lists everything out to her. She explains to him that he is wearing me out, although his intentions are good. She explains to him that at this point, the water hydrotherapy on the treadmill is going to determine most when I will walk again. She orders Joe to cease all other activities except stretching, flexing my leg muscles, bending my joints, and being wheeled outside in the four-wheel carriage to briefly relieve myself. She wants me to be fresh for my next appointments. Joe reiterates to her that he is being squeezed at the Lynnwood clinic to end my boarding, and upon my dismal performance in René's presence, he can't possibly bring me home. Dr. Lamp tells Joe to trust the therapy at her clinic and focus on getting me there in fresh condition. He agrees.

Joe arrives at home later that day from Denver. He has his parents' situation fresh on his mind, and René is busy coordinating some wedding plans for Shawn. The wedding is almost two weeks away, and some details have to be changed and ironed out. They discuss his trip then the wedding before finally getting to me.

"I talked with Dr. Lamp regarding your visit with Bubba. I reviewed with her all the additional activities I have been having everyone work with Bubba on, and she is convinced I had exhausted him. I know this was his first visit at her clinic that you witnessed, but you really need to give it another try before forming any decisions," Joe pitches to René.

"I have gone along with you for the past six or seven weeks. You don't even consult with me anymore while you continue to make decisions to extend his treatment and additional cost. Now I finally witness firsthand whether he is progressing or not, and you want me to not believe what my own eyes are seeing. I can't just blindly go along and support you! I spoke to Dr. Lamp too. Bubba is the worst case she has ever attempted to rehabilitate. Lynnwood is about to force you out the door. You have nowhere for Bubba to go, and he can't come here in his crippled state. I can't care for him," René says, summarizing her frustrations.

"Leave Lynnwood to me. I can handle them," Joe barks back.

"Well, you need to. They wanted me to confirm with them that you would have Bubba moved by this weekend," she answers.

"What did you say? You didn't agree with that, did you?" he asks her.

"I told them you would call them when you get back in town. You are back, so give them a call, but remember, he cannot come here," René states seriously to Joe. She knows if she doesn't stand her ground firmly on this, Joe will come marching through the front door carrying me home.

Joe doesn't want to give in on this point to René, but he is at a loss for words to make a case for me and feeling very trapped with no options. "I am going to go find a place for my dog and myself. I am not giving up on him, and you need to think this through and be prepared to cowboy up with some support," Joe answers in frustration as he is at a loss for words. Joe leaves, taking a bag of clothes, and rents a hotel room for the next few nights.

Joe stops by the Lynnwood clinic and reviews with the staff the strict regimen he wants me on to allow full focus on my water hydrotherapy treatment. He also stalls them on moving me out. He tells them he has a kennel being built for me at his home that isn't ready yet. I have two upcoming treatments, one two days from now and one three days after that. Joe brings me to the next one, and with the rest from my other activities, my performance on the treadmill is much better. You see, with each passing day, my body is healing, even my left side, little by little. Joe kneels down next to me, burying his head close to mine, and whispers, "If only René could have seen you today versus the other day."

Joe goes back home again after two nights in the hotel. René and Joe discuss things and realize they have a lot going on and feel that no matter what, they need to somehow work together. They have been married for some twenty-six years, and this isn't the first time their marriage has been tested with adversity. Joe agrees to be more open-minded and realistic with regards to me, and she agrees to take another look. René explains to him that it is emotionally sapping her strength trying to get her hopes up for me only to have reality set in that we may have to put me to sleep, anyway. It is good they clear the air again. However, I have another water therapy session coming up in a few days, and Joe needs to leave town again for work in California. Shawn will be bringing me to Ballard from Lynnwood, but he wants René to attend as well.

Joe stops by right before he leaves town on his business work trip to talk to me. Here is kind of how it goes.

"Bubba, we have come a long way together in this process. However, I need you to step up and put your game face on. You have me doing all the heavy lifting, so to speak. Your next doctor visit needs to be the high point of your recovery. We are running out of time here in Lynnwood, and your mom won't be letting me bring you home unless a miracle happens. If we were playing poker, I have just moved all my chips to the center of the table. We are all in here, buddy. Sissy, Shawn, will be coming by to pick you up for your big day. Give it your best, and I will see you this weekend."

Then he pats me on my head, gives me a hug, and takes off.

He then calls Dr. Lamp and explains to her he will not be in attendance on my next visit and that Shawn will be bringing me, with René coming too.

"Hey, Doc, it's Joe. I have Shawn bringing Bubba up for his next visit from Lynnwood. Additionally, René will be coming over too. I have a business trip to California I must go on and cannot be there. The reason I am calling is to give you a heads-up on my home situation. As you know, Bubba has been in recovery away from home for almost two months. The bills are mounting for his care, and you can see at what level his progress is at," Joe explains to Dr. Lamp.

"Joe, we are starting to make progress with him," she says as Joe cuts her off.

"Let me just cut to the chase. René and I are a little apart right now on Bubba. I have made the last few decisions on proceeding with him on my own because I knew she would have fought me on things. This has resulted in a disagreement, to say it lightly, and I have moved out into a hotel on a few occasions for a few nights. To say the least, things are a little strained. You get the picture? I need this next visit to go really good," Joe says, giving Dr. Lamp an insight to his home life and marriage.

"I know your family has a lot going on, but I didn't realize to what degree," she responds, acknowledging him.

"Listen, we are a tight family, and even with all we have on our plate right now, we pretty much will stick together. I just need to convince my wife that I am not loony tunes when it comes to Bubba walking again and soon. If she believes he is not a lost cause, she will support me on his recovery and therapy. So I am calling you to make sure you know the importance of this next visit."

"I understand. Make sure he is rested," she emphasizes.

"Aye, aye, sir, you got it," he answers.

Now Joe has everyone on board. The stage is set. Shawn will be picking me up. The Lynnwood staff will make sure I am rested. René will be meeting us in Ballard, and Dr. Lamp knows how important my next visit is to the Flynn family. I hope I can do well.

CHAPTER 20

Walk Again, Showtime?

It is around eleven o'clock on a Thursday morning in late August, and Shawn is here at the Lynnwood vet clinic to pick me up and transport me to Sunrise Vet in Ballard, where René will be meeting us. They lay me in the back of Joe's truck inside the rear enclosed canopy area. He has a rubber floor with a nice, cushioned dog mat for me to lie on. I am rather rambunctious from the last three days of rest but very excited to be with Shawn.

Upon our arrival in Ballard, Dr. Lamp, René, and Jen are standing in front of Sunrise Vet waiting as Shawn parks Joe's truck in the loading/drop-off zone next to them. I am sure happy to see everybody, and I attempt to stand in the back of the truck then fall over but stand back up and lean against the wall of the truck. My legs are a bit wobbly, but boy, am I excited!

Dr. Lamp has a special harness she and Jen are slipping around me that loops around each of my legs and then connects together in the center of my back. Dr. Lamp and Jen then move me down onto the sidewalk, and Dr. Lamp attaches a leash to my new harness. By grabbing the handle on the center of the harness, Dr. Lamp can easily raise me up into a standing position on all four of my legs. She relaxes the support she is giving me, and I stand, a little shaky, but upright. Dr. Lamp proceeds to take a few small steps slowly, lightly tugging at the leash. I attempt to take a few forward steps and meander to the right then the left before lying down on the sidewalk.

Shawn and René are standing off to the side with looks of hope and anticipation on their faces. It is as if they are each watching their baby try to walk for the first time. Dr. Lamp eases me back up into the standing position by pulling up on the center of the harness. She attempts for the second time to begin a slow, steady walk. I gradually start to follow her, take two or three steps, turn my head to look at René and Shawn, and meander off-balance. There I lie on the sidewalk again.

Shawn comes over and speaks to Dr. Lamp. They both nod in agreement. Shawn goes to the other side of the truck and opens the rear door, taking something out. Dr. Lamp gets my attention and assists me in standing up to make ready for my next attempt. Dr. Lamp gives me the "Stay" command, as if I were going to take off, when Shawn walks out in front of us, placing a scented decoy birdie on the center of the sidewalk thirty feet away. Shawn walks back to Dr. Lamp and lets me smell the scent of decoy birdie that is lingering on her fingers. Shawn is not a bird hunter; however, she did go with Joe and me on several occasions, taking pictures of my hunting in the field. She knows all the commands to have me stay, release, fetch, or hunt. Before leaving town, Joe had scented decoy birdie and put it in a sealed bag in the back seat of his truck, with instructions for Shawn to use it to motivate me.

Shawn releases me to go fetch decoy birdie, and I bolt clumsily forward, pulling Dr. Lamp down the sidewalk. The scent is getting stronger with each step I take. I have one thing on my mind, to pick up decoy birdie and return it to Shawn. Both of my eyes are focused on birdie while the leash is pulled taut in the hand of Dr. Lamp, who is struggling to keep up with me. Finally, we arrive at decoy birdie. I pick it up, turn to the right, stagger briefly, and pull Dr. Lamp down the sidewalk to return decoy birdie to Shawn. René and Shawn are smiling from ear to ear, with tears rolling down their cheeks. They both hug and congratulate me for fetching decoy birdie. What I haven't realized is that I clumsily, but strongly, pulled Dr. Lamp successfully down the sidewalk under my own power.

Dr. Lamp says, "Let us try that again."

This time, she has me stay while she instructs Shawn to place decoy birdie a good sixty feet down the sidewalk. I have the scent strongly captured within the portholes of my nose. The aroma is overwhelming all my senses, putting me in full hunting mode. The endorphins are going off throughout my body. Shawn releases me, and I bolt down the sidewalk, with Dr. Lamp in tow. Midway there, I stumble to the right, recover quickly on my own, and complete the distance. I scoop up decoy birdie and head back toward Shawn and return birdie. Upon another successful retrieval, I again receive accolades and hugs from both René and Shawn. They are both laughing, wishing that Joe could have been here to see for himself.

Dr. Lamp has an idea and wants to bring me inside to the water tank. I want to stay outside and play decoy-birdie-fetch, but I am not the one running the show. Dr. Lamp has Jen get me ready to go into the water tank for a hydrotherapy session on the treadmill. They only fill the tank with about half as much water as I am used to having and have me in the tank by myself. They hit the switch to start the treadmill, which forces me to start walking. Dr. Lamp then puts decoy birdie in front of me, but on the other side of the glass door, while increasing the speed of the treadmill. I want to get to decoy birdie, but no matter how fast I attempt to walk on the treadmill, decoy birdie is always a step away. Now that I look back and think about it, Dr. Lamp's hand on the dial of the treadmill speed control may have had something to do with it.

Dr. Lamp keeps me on the treadmill for close to six minutes of steadily walking my partially buoyant, paralyzed body into exhaustion. Finally, we stop. It is my best workout performance to date at Sunrise Vet. After I have been cleaned up, Jen walks me out to the truck. While in my new harness, I stop next to a tree, lift my leg, and pee like a regular dog. René's and Shawn's mouths drop open. Besides walking today, it paints a picture in René's mind that I am capable of relieving myself without having to be carried or assisted in anyway.

After peeing, Jen tries to walk me in the harness with the leash to the truck, but exhaustion is rapidly crawling over my whole body. I lazily lie down on the sidewalk, unable to continue to the truck.

Jen tries to raise me up by pulling up on the center of the harness; however, my body will not respond. All the motivation and endorphins have now exited my system, leaving me completely exhausted. Shawn and Jen roll me onto the stretcher and load me into the back of the truck.

The good thing is, my earlier performance has won the day. I've exceeded everyone's expectations with my sidewalk fetching and my water tank performance. René and Shawn have called Joe to tell him, but he is involved in some big meeting to save his company and doesn't answer the call.

René thanks Dr. Lamp for her help after discussing firsthand with her my prognosis for the future. Shawn and René have lunch together close by the clinic to celebrate the day's success while I drift into a deep sleep in the back of Joe's truck, comfortably, on my cushioned blanket.

We find out later that Joe intentionally didn't take the call from René because he wanted to speak with Dr. Lamp first. He was afraid of getting bad news. Joe calls Dr. Lamp and asks how everything went.

"Dr. Lamp, it's me. I am on pins and needles, wanting to know how things went today with Bubba." He anxiously awaits her response.

Dr. Lamp, with tears in her eyes at the other end of the phone line, begins to describe to Joe the day's events. "Joe, it couldn't have been scripted better in a Hollywood movie. Bubba was fantastic, and you having Shawn bring decoy birdie to focus and motivate him was excellent. He literally pulled me on a leash down the sidewalk a good thirty feet the first time, then sixty feet the second time, fetching decoy birdie. René, Shawn, Jen, and I were laughing and crying at the same time. We were all so happy for him! It was unbelievable, more than what I would have expected."

Joe sits stunned in a proud silence at the other end of the phone. "I don't know what to say. I can't tell you how happy I am. It has been such a long road without much positive progress. This is such a breakthrough!"

"René and Shawn left here extremely pleased with Bubba's progress. You shouldn't have to be renting any more hotel rooms on Bubba's account. Call René as soon as you get a chance and rejoice in the good news together. You both deserve it!" Dr. Lamp kids with Joe.

"I will do that once I hang up. Thanks so much. I am so glad I found your clinic." Joe signs off graciously.

"Oh, before you run off, I will call Lynnwood for you and see if I can buy you a little more time while you figure out your home situation for Bubba. Call me tomorrow. I need some time to gather my thoughts and come up with a revised game plan for Bubba," Dr. Lamp says, ending the conversation. Then Dr. Lamp calls Lynnwood and extends my stay by one more week. Now, Joe calls René, and they share in the good news together.

"Hey, it's me. I just got off the phone with a pretty ecstatic Dr. Lamp. What did you think about his performance today?" Joe excitedly inquires of his wife.

"Your dog had me at hello today." René laughs back over the phone to her husband. "Not only did your dog do phenomenal, but Dan just called from Iraq. He is safe and expecting to be able to come home for Shawn and Brent's wedding."

"Oh, honey, that's great!" Joe concurs with her.

"Listen, we will figure Bubba out somehow. He had a really good day today. Dr. Lamp's therapy is really outstanding, cutting edge," she says.

René is convinced that I can eventually walk again, maybe even run, based upon my performance today. Additionally, with Dan calling from Iraq, knowing he is okay and safe really puts a positive accent on the day's events! Joe hangs up the phone and is really happy. He could not have hoped for better news regarding me if he wrote it himself, and now both Joe and René know their son is safe too. In the back of his mind, when René said, "He might even be able to run again," Joe pictures us hunting again, but no, that won't be possible.

The next day, Joe calls and speaks with Dr. Lamp regarding yesterday's events surrounding my performance and how we may best affect my progress. She notes that my walking gait is stiff. I am able to successfully transport myself down the sidewalk and back, but I am not effectively bending my legs at the joints. Dr. Lamp feels that if we insert stair-climbing into my training rehab regimen, this will accomplish two things: Force me to bend my legs at the joints versus carrying them more stiffly when on level ground. I am having a tendency to swing my legs out to the side in a sort of shuffle. The second thing is that stair-climbing will build back my leg muscles, which have been primarily inactive the last two months. She tells Joe to cut back on the swimming and replace it with stair-climbing. It will be necessary for Joe to assist me in accomplishing this feat by using my new harness.

She comments to Joe that when I am motivated by the scented hunting decoy, it is like I am a dog on steroids. I am definitely a more energized dog when I am focused on the hunting decoy. She wants to continue to try to channel this focused energy into my training rehab whenever possible. Joe explains to her that whenever he starts to gather his gear to take me hunting, I will follow him through the house and garage, anxiously waiting to get put into his truck to be taken to the field. Once at the field, during the fifteen to twenty minutes we have to wait for the field to open at eight o'clock in the morning, I howl and bark with anticipation. However, after a day's hunting, I come down hard and go into a deep sleep from the day's activity.

Dr. Lamp comments on my left front leg. This leg is the worst affected by the FCE stroke. I want to kind of keep it curled back. This causes me to drag the top of it on the ground before actually flipping it forward so that it lands on the paw pad. During my first six hydrotherapy sessions, Dr. Lamp is in the water tank with me, moving my front legs. She has to teach me how to flip this still partially paralyzed left front leg forward so that I can begin to use it again. She comments that when I am excited and focused on the decoy bird, I pick the leg up and thrust it forward. When I am just lazily trying to walk, I have a tendency to drag the leg along the ground. Once again, she feels the stair-climbing will force me to bend the leg at the joint versus shuffling a stiff leg.

Joe is still in California when Shawn comes to visit me in Lynnwood the next day. Everyone there has heard the good news about me when Dr. Lamp called to extend my stay for another week. However, no one can get me to move today. I am exhausted from yesterday's activities. My legs are stiff, weak, and sore. *Give me an anti-inflammatory and let me sleep.* Except, I can smell a hamburger emanating from Shawn. I drowsily pick my head up to greet her and gently wag my tail. She rubs and pats me while I groan.

She says, "You are pretty tired today. I guess I shouldn't make you work for this hamburger."

Music to my ears!

I drool in anticipation, and Shawn gives me the burger. The technicians tell Shawn they have tried to take me outside this morning in my carriage to go to the bathroom but I am like a soft, wet noodle.

In my present physical condition, it will take me twenty-four to thirty-six hours to completely recover from any type of workout. I have experienced no muscle atrophy, but my leg muscles are out of shape from inactivity and still partially paralyzed. The recovery time will continue to get shorter over time, though.

CHAPTER 21

Stair-Climbing

Joe arrives home from work in California. The next day, when he comes to Lynnwood for work, he comes in to see me. This is my lucky day, as he is taking me out to a local park to lie in the grass and smell the outdoors like a normal dog. It is my reward for doing well at Dr. Lamp the other day. There are some railroad tie wooden steps at the park forming a gradual grassy landing as you ascend each step. There are six gradual steps. I am wearing my new harness, which makes it easy for Joe to pull up on the handle, raising me to the standing position and assisting me to walk. Dr. Lamp gives Joe strict orders to go slow and not overdo it.

We begin by approaching the steps. I look up and wonder if Joe actually wants me to attempt to pull my legs up and walk up each one. I am still struggling to walk on level ground. He nudges me by pulling forward on the handle. I try to shuffle and stiff-leg it. He helps me climb the first step. Then he moves me in order that my front legs are directly in front of the railroad tie of the second step. Now to get my front legs on top of the second step, I am going to have to bend my legs at the joints. I try to back up so that I can shuffle myself up, but Joe controls the handle on my harness. He helps me bend one of my legs, and we move up to the second step.

Joe says, "Bubba, you are a smart dog. We need to practice this stair-climbing with you being focused and motivated." He has me stay on the landing of the second step while he places a small dog bone treat on the sixth step of the landing. He comes back, grabs the handle on my harness, and gives a small tug forward. We ascend the remaining four steps to the dog bone treat. I bang some of my paws on the front of the wooden tie steps and may have even tripped; however, Joe's hand on the harness guides me to the top.

We go back to the bottom and perform this exercise at least five more times, with the dog bone treat at the top of the last step of the landing. I am panting, and my legs are tired. Joe walks me back to his truck with assistance, and we return to the Lynnwood facility. We perform the stairs in the local park four times over the next week and a half along with three hydrotherapy sessions in Ballard with Dr. Lamp. I am beginning to bend my legs at the joints, and I am steadily getting stronger. My endurance is increasing.

Joe explains the level of stair-climbing we are doing at the park to Dr. Lamp. She feels it is time for me to attempt more stairs and possibly be brought home to do the stairs in our house. Rather than bring me home for good, she feels it will be a good idea to bring me home for a few hours, stair-climb, and let me lie in the front yard. It will get me used to the house and get René familiar with seeing me at the house again.

At this point in my rehabilitation, I can walk a short distance if assisted and guided by someone with a leash attached to the center of my harness. I am still a bit shaky if I attempt it on my own. Additionally, I can only walk on grass, concrete, cement, or a carpeted surface. If you put me on a wooden or linoleum floor, my legs will slide and slip out from under me. All four legs will sprawl out to the sides until my body hits the deck. Joe and René's house has carpeted stairs and rooms; however, the hallways connecting the rooms are wooden floors, much too slippery for me to walk on. The garage floor is concrete; however, its surface is really smooth with a slippery coating. I cannot walk on the garage floor. The good thing about bringing me home for this two-hour visit, it gives Joe and René a good idea as to the difficulties I am going to have. They are both committed to finding a way to make it work. It is like bringing a handicapped person home from the hospital for the first time and you realizing how you have to make changes to accommodate the handicapped person. Joe brings me into the house by coming through the rear bottom door. We enter through the main TV room downstairs, which is carpeted and leads to the carpeted steps to go upstairs to the main floor. There are about eight steps to reach the landing, then a turn to the left, and another ten steps to reach the main floor. These steps are steep, with no landing on each step, and more in number than what I am used to.

Joe puts a small dog treat bone on the landing and another at the top on the main floor. We begin. I am excited to be home, so my adrenaline is running on high. We ascend the first steps, grab the dog treat, then head up to the main floor. Joe is helping me just enough to steady me while allowing me to do most of the work. We repeat this until I make three complete ascensions. I am tired. Joe tells me we have ten total ascensions before we finish, and he wants me to try it without the dog treats. We do two more, and now I am exhausted. We take a break and get a drink of water, and Joe reintroduces the dog treats back, only this time there is only one treat at the very top. We work through five more ascensions to total ten, and I am pooped.

Joe and René have their lawn chairs on the front lawn with Keely girl. I can smell around the yard and easily scent where she has shallowly buried four bones. On my next visit, it is my goal to uncover and find them. For now, I am tired and Joe has a leash on my harness to keep me close to his lawn chair. We sit on the lawn for an hour, and it feels good to be home.

"Well, what do you think, honey? Can we make this work so I can bring my best friend home?" Joe looks over at René with a boyish grin.

"I suppose so, as you two seem to be inseparable and Bubba sure has earned it." René smiles back.

Then Joe loads me up into the truck and brings me back to Lynnwood, where I am stashed away in my blockaded little area. Joe lets me know he will be getting me out of here real soon.

CHAPTER 22

Coming Home

Joe buys an eight-by-eight-by-four-foot iron fence kennel with a gate from the pet store. He intends to assemble it on the garage floor on top of sod grass, as the floor is too slippery for me. Instead, René takes him to a carpet warehouse and they buy a piece of carpet big enough to cover the whole garage floor. Joe and Uncle Bob assemble the kennel fence on top of the carpet. At this point, if I stand up and try to walk on my own, I can easily fall over. They want me in an enclosed area to keep me safe. It will be easy from this location to walk me assisted into the front yard from the garage in my harness to relieve myself and get my daily exercise.

The big day comes for me to say goodbye to the Lynnwood staff. All the technicians gather around. They give me a bath, and I smell good. Everyone is excited to see me go but, at the same time, sad too. I hear one of them say, "Sort of bittersweet." In the two months I have been here, I have become a fixture in the place. There are tears welling up in the staff's eyes as they are witnessing the culmination of the successful progress I have achieved under their care. Now, everything is coming to a conclusion. Jennifer hugs me the tightest of all.

Joe walks through the door with my new harness. Remember, the floors in Lynnwood are linoleum, too slippery for me to try to walk on, but Joe thinks it fitting for me to walk out with his assistance. The technicians have tears freely flowing down their cheeks as we begin our slow walk out of the clinic to the truck outside. They think back over the last two months how, with their help and dedication, I have overcome insurmountable odds. I truly was a lost cause from the get-go, but somehow, everyone stuck by me, did their part, and didn't quit on me. These guys see an enormous amount of tragedy and death in their emergency line of work. They have to try to separate themselves from it, or it will pull them down. If they allow this to happen, they will not be ready for their next case. I am one they had to become attached to; I needed their commitment for these last two months, or I wouldn't have made it. We are now outside, and Joe is loading me into the back of his truck. I stand up in the back of the truck and bark at the staff. Joe is shaking all their hands, thanking each one individually.

Jennifer reaches into the back of the open truck canopy and hugs me again. "I am sure going to miss you, Bubba!" Tears are flowing down her face while the other technicians all clap, giving me an applause sendoff.

Joe tells them, "You are truly professionals, each and every one, and without your extraordinary effort, Bubba would not have made it. It is hard for me to find the right words to say to express my gratitude to all of you." He promises to keep in touch with them and keep them informed about my future progress. Everyone waves goodbye as we drive out of the parking lot for the last time.

A short time later, we arrive home. René and Shawn are in the driveway. Keely and Benji are barking in the front yard. Joe lifts me out of the truck and steadies me by holding my harness. I walk onto the front lawn to greet Keely and Benji. Shawn has made a nice big sign that says, "Welcome Home, Bubba!" She then puts Keely and Benji in the house while René hugs and pets me. She tells me, "It is sure good to have you back here."

I am excited to be home to all my familiar places, my smells, but most of all, my family. I walk slowly around the front yard, urinate on one of my favorite spots, and smell one of Keely's bones tucked under a bush. I grab it, lie down in the grass, and start chewing. René, Shawn, and Joe pull up lawn chairs next to me. Joe looks over at René and Shawn and proceeds to thank them for all their help and support. It has been a team effort throughout.

Joe says, "I didn't think we would get to this day. Truly amazing! Now, is someone here ready to get married this coming weekend?"

"Dad, if we can accomplish this with Bubba, the wedding will be a piece of cake," Shawn replies.

Joe checks with them on the wedding plans, and both René and Shawn confirm all is okay. The wedding is only four days away. One of our neighbors even volunteers to watch over me on the wedding day.

The next day, I am in my garage kennel, with the garage door up, when a car pulls up. It is René's friend Kate. She has not seen me in almost two months since her visit to Lynnwood when I was first injured. When I see her, I stand up in my carpeted kennel, start wagging my tail, and give her a big *woof* hello. She immediately has tears running down her face, with a big smile going from ear to ear. She says, "Bubba, you are one lucky dog!" She squeezes me tight and pets me.

The wedding goes off without a hitch. It is a memorable occasion for the whole family, especially for Shawn and Brent, the two newlyweds. They are off to Hawaii for their honeymoon, and we have a house guest, Benji. Keely and Benji get to stay in the house while I bunk up in the garage in my new, carpeted kennel.

My new regimen is for René or Joe to let me out into the front yard morning, noon, and night for monitored exercise in my harness. I walk around and relieve myself. I need assistance to squat back for a bowel movement. My legs are not strong enough to accomplish this yet. When I first attempted to squat back, I ended up rolling back, doing a backward somersault. Since then, Joe or René holds on to the harness in the center of my back to assist me. After two weeks of their assistance, I am strong enough to perform this feat on my own. An exercise period lasts about fifteen to twenty minutes, enough to allow me to strengthen my legs but not exhaust myself. Joe stair-climbs me in the house, and he still brings me to Sunrise Vet twice per week, once on a weekday and once on the weekend.

I've been home four weeks. I am able to walk on my own in the front yard without the harness or assistance. René buys throw rugs for the wooden floors inside the house. This allows me to come inside, except the door that leads downstairs has to be closed. I am not strong enough to ascend or descend the stairs safely on my own yet. They have to watch and make sure Keely doesn't knock me over. Joe is taking me to the park or on the local trail system in his truck for exercise. I cannot run up the dog ramp to enter the back of his truck like I used to; he has to pick me up. By going to the park, I am able to walk in the forest, which forces me to pick up my legs and bend my joints to successfully clear fallen branches. Steadily my legs are becoming more agile. Joe finds a grassy hill with a gradual slope to it. He takes me to the bottom of this hill in my harness, and together we ascend it. This further strengthens my legs. Eventually, I can ascend the hill under my own power.

In Joe's absence for work or travel, René cannot take me to the park, as she is too small to lift me into the back of the truck. René thinks that if she has a vehicle with a lower tail end to the ground, she will be able to assist me with my harness on. She buys a used blue PT Cruiser with custom license plates that say, "4 Bubba." The family nicknames it the Bubbamobile. It is used mainly to transport me to and from the park for exercise.

CHAPTER 23

The Big Test

My recovery, to date, for normal walking is 75 percent on my right side and 60 percent on my left side. If I am excited, you can increase these percentages for a short time by about 20 percent. On this occasion, Joe brings me to the park. We walk on the trails through the trees, allowing me to smell all my familiar spots. I relieve myself, remarking some old territory. It is evening, the lights are on, and the soccer field is empty. The field is level, covered in Astro grass, which means there are no worn, slippery spots for me to slip on. Joe has me stay while he puts decoy birdie thirty yards down the middle of the field. I have not seen decoy birdie since my big day outside of Dr. Lamp's office. He still has some leftover scent on him. The endorphins are going off in my body as I click into hunting mode. Joe releases me. I break into a galloping run down the soccer field, with my eyes riveted on decoy birdie. I gently snatch him up into my mouth and run back to Joe. I prance in front of him as I drop decoy birdie at his feet. He hugs me and says, "You never cease to amaze me, Bubba!"

I want to do more, but he leashes me up and brings me home. Later that week, he brings me to see Dr. Lamp and tells her about the encounter on the soccer field motivated by decoy birdie. They discuss the idea of allowing me to hunt again. It is autumn, and we are right smack in the middle of pheasant-hunting season.

"Bubba is strong. He has a gait abnormality when he walks, displaying a slight limp, but when motivated, he seems to have an increased ability to walk and even run. Walking in the field will give him good practice to pick up his legs to get over fallen tree branches and the like. Don't let him overdo it. You must understand he will never be the dog he used to be," Dr. Lamp says.

She gives Joe the okay. "Keep it to within an hour and choose the terrain accordingly. Try to go when there will be a minimum of other hunters and dogs."

There is no dog on record getting a second canine FCE stroke; however, there aren't many, if any, dogs that have survived such an extreme stroke either. Joe has Dr. Lamp's permission to take me on a short monitored hunt, but he doesn't have René's permission. This is going to be interesting to see how Joe goes about bringing this subject up to René and gets her to say yes. Now, mind you, I want to go, but that is beside the point. This whole family, with the work of professionals, has sacrificed a lot to get me back just so I can live a normal life again.

Joe has two lawn chairs on the front grass for him and René to sit and enjoy the evening.

"Hey, guess what? I was talking with Dr. Lamp, and she thought it would be a good idea for me to take Bubba on a short small, little pheasant hunt." Joe strategically lets the cat out of the bag.

"A what? Are you serious?" René asks.

"Well, she sees how motivated he gets with decoy birdie and knows actual hunting would motivate him even more. He needs to continue to learn to bend his legs at the joints and maneuver over uneven terrain. She told me to keep it short and go on a day when hardly anyone else would be out there." Joe quickly gets the right words out. He is a sly one, my master.

"Don't even get me started on how we all worked so hard to get Bubba back to where he is at. I would hate to see you cause him a relapse," René cautions.

"It won't be much more than me taking him to the park. I will choose the right place based on the terrain, nothing too difficult for him, and keep it short, according to Dr. Lamp's instructions," he responds.

René isn't happy and enthusiastic about Joe taking me, but she knows we both love to hunt. She tells him to be extra careful. I am excited—tomorrow morning, we will be going hunting again.

CHAPTER **24**

Hunting Again

I t is a weekday morning, a workday for most folks, so there will not be many hunters in the field. We are up early, and I follow Joe around the garage while he gathers his hunting gear into his truck. He can tell I am excited, because every few minutes, I bark at him. *Why is he taking so long to load up his stuff?* He tells me, "Don't you get too excited. This is going to be a short trip." Finally, all is ready, and off we drive.

Joe always stops for his coffee and a doughnut on our way out into the fields. Today is no different, except it is our first time out this year. The coffee barista sees Joe in his hunter orange shirt and hat, and she asks, "I haven't seen you this year?"

I slip my head out the back window of the canopy and bark.

She says, "Looks like somebody is raring to go."

Joe says, "Yes, this is his favorite thing to do. Just been a busy year, and this is our first time out."

We arrive at the field twenty minutes early. There is only one other hunter and dog in the parking lot. Joe lifts me down from the back of his truck as he unfolds his chair. He always sits in a folding chair next to his truck to drink his coffee. I sniff around the lot in the general vicinity of his truck, relieve myself, then sit next to him while we wait for the time to strike eight o'clock sharp. It looks like we will have the south side of the field all to ourselves. The terrain

125

is a flat marshy field with tall grass and some fallen branches, but no deep gullies for me to fall into. Joe says, "Let's go."

We start into the field, and I can immediately smell weak scents of pheasant that are a few hours to a day old—nothing fresh. I walk slowly and methodically, smelling the area. My old method was to gallop through the tall grass, streaking from side to side, until I came upon a fresh scent. Then follow that scent until I knew we were upon it. Today, I am just glad to be out here. After twenty minutes, we come to the end of the field and start to work our way back to the middle.

Suddenly, I come upon a fresh pheasant scent. My tail goes straight up in the air, circling, and I pick up my step. Joe notices immediately that I am on to something. I go back and forth through the tall grass as the scent meanders through the brush. My energy level excels through my whole body. I trip over some fallen branches, roll in the grass, and get right back to my feet and continue to track the scent. Now we are just in the tall thick marsh grass. I circle the scent as I glance back at Joe. This is my signal to him. I hear, "Birdie, Bubba!" I pounce with my front paws, mostly my right paw, on the grass directly in front of me. A colorful male rooster pheasant flies up into the air to the left then darts quickly to the right. Joe fires twice with his shotgun, but today is the rooster's lucky day. He flies away across the field back into the woods.

I turn and look at Joe, thinking, *That was a lot of work for nothing.* I give him the dumb-dog look. *Why didn't that bird fall?* He tells me I did really good and performed my job well. I am intent on finding another one, but Joe wants to take me back to the truck. I can't understand why he seems so happy about this hunting excursion—he missed his shot. What I don't know is what he is thinking inside to himself. He is flashing back to midsummer, when I was helplessly struggling on the floor of the Lynnwood clinic. He couldn't imagine then that this coming fall season, we would be out in the field, hunting again. He brings me home, gives me an anti-inflammatory, and lets me rest.

René asks, "How did things go?"

Joe proudly tells how well I performed in the field and how poorly his aim was. René always likes to hear when some of the birds get to fly away.

Joe goes off to work.

Later that afternoon, René calls Joe and says, "Bubba hasn't moved since you left for work. He is lying in front of the fireplace, sleeping."

I am really tired. I guess with my new-rehabbed body, any real physical exercise I do causes me to really come down. I get sore, stiff, and tired, requiring me to sleep for a good day.

The next morning, Joe and René are having coffee in the kitchen when I stand up and wag my tail. I am refreshed again. "Well, look who is back after a good night's sleep," Joe says. Joe will take note of my progress and recovery time over the ensuing months. I continue to get stronger, but I always will have an abnormal gait. The partial stiffness to my left side is permanent.

It snows heavily on Christmas. There is a foot of snow in the front yard. I am able to walk around in it. I always love rolling in wet white snow, and this will be no different. Keely joins me. She loves the snow too. Joe and René look out through the front glass window with their lighted Christmas tree in the background. Life is good again. It is really nice to be home.

E P I L O G U E

I t has been four years since Bubba had his canine FCE stroke. He is nine years old. He asked me to write the epilogue to this dog story, and it is an honor for me to do so. Bubba has always been a great family pet and an avid hunting partner in the field. Since coming home from his FCE stroke in September 2006, he has continued to get stronger. We went on a few more short hunts in November 2006 where we successfully bagged a few pheasant for the dinner table. In the spring of 2007, he had the first of three relapses, whereby he would just lie on the floor and not want to be touched for twenty-four to forty-eight hours. His left side would seem to stiffen up. We treated this symptom with pain medication and anti-inflammatory pills. Then as quickly as it came on, it would be gone, like it never happened. It has been over a year since his third relapse occurred, so hopefully relapses are in the rearview mirror for the remainder of his life.

By the summer of 2007, Bubba was able to walk up to two miles in one outing. Over a year after his recovery for the pheasant-hunting season of October and November of 2007, he was able to hunt for a two-hour period, moving in and out of gullies, over uneven terrain. He was a slower, more methodical hunting dog compared to his preinjury years. Back then, he would cover an enormous amount of territory in a fast manner. He was just as effective finding pheasant in this new, slower style because his most powerful weapon, his nose, was still 100 percent. We didn't hunt very much in 2007, as I needed to attend to my mother and father. My mom passed away in September 2007 due to complications from Alzheimer's disease, and

129

my father passed away in February 2008 also due to complications from Alzheimer's disease. My dad always loved to pet Bubba when he stayed or visited us before his death. Bubba always sits next to me, even to this day, when others are in the room, with the exception of my father. For the short time my dad was with us during the fall of 2007, Bubba loved to lay his head on my dad's lap. He seemed to know Dad wasn't going to be with us much longer.

One year later, in the fall of 2008, it was the last year I took Bubba consistently hunting. He seemed even stronger than the year before. I had resigned from my job, and we both had plenty of time on our hands. We hunted three to four times a week. We spent hours in the woods, forests, and banks of the river together, enjoying our passion.

It is now the spring of 2010, and he has slowed down over the last year and half.

Our biggest hunts now are in the yard or at the park. He waits while I go hide decoy birdie, then I come back and release him. No matter where I hide it, he always finds it. When looking for decoy birdie, he has an extra speed to his step. When walking in the yard or around the house, he walks with a noticeable limp. I have had countless evenings sitting and watching the news, a movie, or a sporting event on television with Bubba lying at my feet. If I get up to get something, he follows me through our house. René calls him my shadow.

He truly is my best friend. We have been through much together. He announces whenever I pull into the driveway with his welcoming bark, even though it has faded over the years. René and I have moved to Montana for three months to write this book and to see our son, Dan, and his wife, Ashley, before they deploy to Afghanistan. Bubba loves the house we are in. It is late in the spring of 2010 in Montana. Gophers dig holes in the open fields that surround our house. Bubba is starting to figure out that chasing a gopher in one hole doesn't necessarily mean he won't come out another hole. Once a day, around five o'clock in the afternoon, we go out and play decoy birdie. He lies behind the wheel of my truck to blind him while I go hide decoy birdie in the grass of the field next to the stream.

He will continue to be my friend with the remaining years of life he has left. I will always look at him as the miracle dog.

A C K N O W L E D G E M E N T S

O n Bubba's behalf and mine, I want to acknowledge all the professionals involved with his recovery or rehabilitation. I will list
sequentially, in chronological order, in which they came into Bubba's
life. There was my neighbor Mark, a veterinarian, who first assisted
in calling Redmond Hill Vet Clinic while he helped me lift and strap
Bubba to the dog ramp. The doctor at Redmond Hill Vet Clinic who
mentioned the injury could possibly be neuro-related and suggested
Lynnwood Vet Center; the Lynnwood doctors and technicians, for
their proper diagnosis of the injury, the way in which they painted the
potential picture, and the road to recovery. Their daily, round-the-
clock diligence to caring and treating Bubba, the above and beyond
involvement of themselves in taking Bubba's case as a personal quest
toward his recovery, and especially, the technician Jennifer, whose
impassioned plea to give it just a little more time proved to be mon-
umental. Her personal recommendation and brochure for Sunrise
Vet Clinic was both vital and timely. Dr. Lamp's vision, years before
Bubba's injury, recognized the need for rehabilitation in canine therapy. Her and her staff's professionalism and expertise in teaching
paralyzed, crippled canines how to walk again.

Uncle Bob, for all the trips he made to Lake Washington, helping carry Bubba from the parking lot to the water. Also for helping
me build the welcome-home kennel in our garage for Bubba. Bubba
wants to thank Uncle Bob for all the times he came hunting with us
too.

My family, for persevering through the emotional ups and
downs, mostly downs, of Bubba's phenomenal recovery and rehab.

My wife, René, forced me to focus and apply reason to a difficult situation; however, she was always there to support or help when it counted.

My daughter Shawn's almost-daily support with Bubba. We worked together then, and she could see Bubba daily to assist me. For her impassioned and timely plea to stay the course for just a little bit longer, giving Bubba the extra needed time to heal and show progress.

My son, Dan, sent emails from Iraq, wanting to know Bubba's status and that we would not give up on him.

If a link in this chain weakened and broke at any time during Bubba's recovery, this would not have been a successful comeback story. To all listed here, Bubba and I want to thank you.

In closing, to see someone, whether a person or a dog, pick himself off the floor against insurmountable odds and recover through intense rehab therapy to have a life again is truly amazing to witness firsthand. I can say this because I have seen it. I hope I have been able to convey and portray this incredible story to you in a manner in which you can appreciate it. If this book is successful, it is my goal to set aside a portion of profits to the treatment of canines in need.

Sincerely,
Joe Flynn

B efore becoming a Seattle native after four years in the USMC, the author met his wife, René, in Seattle, and they have been married for over thirty-five years, with a beautiful family. They currently reside in Montana.

He started work in the mailroom of a company and quickly moved his way up into senior management positions through perseverance, commitment, and hard work. Always a dog owner and passionate about everything he does, he was forced to decide the fate of his beloved dog, Bubba.

Never one to give up, and with numerous obstacles to overcome, Joe believed he could succeed.

In the outdoors, he loves hiking, fishing, and bird-hunting. Through chance or fate, he became a writer, as he and his dog have a story to tell.

Please join us!

CPSIA information can be obtained
at www.ICGtesting.com
Printed in the USA
LVHW051109040819
626449LV00002B/585

9 781642 149994